The Collected Poetry

MW01284411

Volume II

William Cowper was born 26th November 1731 in Berkhamsted, Hertfordshire. Traumatically he and his brother, John, were the only survivors, out of seven, to survive infancy. His mother died when he was six.

His education, after several temporary schools, was stabilised at Westminster school. Here he established several life-long friendships and a dedication to Latin. Upon leaving he was articled to a solicitor in London and spent almost a decade training in Law. In 1763 he was offered a Clerkship of Journals in the House of Lords. With the examinations approaching Cowper had a mental breakdown. He tried to commit suicide three times and a period of depression and insanity seemed to settle on him. The end of this unhappy period saw him find refuge in fervent evangelical Christianity, and it was also the inspiration behind his much-loved hymns.

This led to a collaboration with John Newton in writing 'Olney Hymns'.

However dark forces were about to overwhelm Cowper. In 1773, he experienced a devastating attack of insanity, believing that he was eternally condemned to hell, and that God was instructing him to make a sacrifice of his own life. With great care and devotion his friend, Mary Unwin, nursed him back to health.

In 1781 Cowper had the good fortune to meet a widow, Lady Austen, who inspired a new bout of poetry writing. Cowper himself tells of the genesis of what some have considered his most substantial work, 'The Task'.

In 1786 he began his translations from the Greek into blank verse of Homer's 'The Iliad' and 'The Odyssey'. These translations, published in 1791, were the most significant since those of Alexander Pope earlier in the century.

Mary Unwin died in 1796, plunging Cowper into a gloom from which he never fully recovered though he did continue to write.

William Cowper was seized with dropsy and died on 25th April 1800.

Index of Contents

PREFACE TO THE POEMS

When an author, by appearing in print, requests an audience of the public, and is upon the point of speaking for himself, whoever presumes to step before him with a preface, and to say, "Nay, but hear me first," should have something worthy of attention to offer, or he will be justly deemed officious and impertinent. The judicious reader has probably, upon other occasions, been beforehand with me in this reflection: and I am not very willing it should now be applied to me, however I may seem to expose myself to the danger of it. But the thought of having my own name perpetuated in connexion with the name in the title-page is so pleasing and flattering to the feelings of my heart, that I am content to risk something for the gratification.

This Preface is not designed to commend the Poems to which it is prefixed. My testimony would be insufficient for those who are not qualified to judge properly for themselves, and unnecessary to those who are. Besides, the reasons which render it improper and unseemly for a man to celebrate his own performances, or those of his nearest relatives, will have some influence in suppressing much of what he might otherwise wish to say in favour of a friend, when that friend is indeed an alter idem, and excites almost the same emotions of sensibility and affection as he feels for himself.

It is very probable these Poems may come into the hands of some persons, in whom the sight of the author's name will awaken a recollection of incidents and scenes, which through length of time they had almost forgotten. They will be reminded of one, who was once the companion of their chosen hours, and who set out with them in early life in the paths which lead to literary honours, to influence and affluence, with equal prospects of success. But he was suddenly and powerfully withdrawn from those pursuits, and he left them without regret; yet not till he had sufficient opportunity of counting the cost, and of knowing the value of what he gave up. If happiness could have been found in classical attainments, in an elegant taste, in the exertions of wit, fancy, and genius, and in the esteem and converse of such persons, as in these respects were most congenial with himself, he would have been happy. But he was not—he wondered (as thousands in a similar situation still do) that he should continue dissatisfied, with all the means apparently conducive to satisfaction within his reach—But in due time the cause of his disappointment was discovered to him—he had lived without God in the world. In a memorable hour, the wisdom which is from above visited his heart. Then he felt himself a wanderer, and then he found a guide. Upon this change of views, a change of plan and conduct followed of course. When he saw the busy and the gay world in its true light, he left it with as little reluctance as a prisoner, when called to liberty, leaves his dungeon. Not that he became a Cynic or an Ascetic—a heart filled with love to God will assuredly breathe benevolence to men. But the turn of his temper inclining him to rural life, he indulged it, and, the providence of God evidently preparing his way and marking out his retreat, he retired into the country. By these steps the good hand of God, unknown to me, was providing for me one of the principal blessings of my life; a friend and a counsellor, in whose company for almost seven years, though we were seldom seven successive waking hours separated, I always found new pleasure—a friend who was not only a comfort to myself, but a blessing to the affectionate poor people among whom I then lived.

Some time after inclination had thus removed him from the hurry and bustle of life, he was still more secluded by a long indisposition, and my pleasure was succeeded by a proportionable degree of anxiety and concern. But a hope, that the God whom he served would support him under his affliction, and at length vouchsafe him a happy deliverance, never forsook me. The desirable crisis, I trust, is now nearly approaching. The dawn, the presage of returning day, is already arrived. He is again enabled to resume his pen, and some of the first fruits of his recovery are here presented to the public. In his principal subjects, the same acumen, which distinguished him in the early period of life, is happily employed in illustrating and enforcing the truths of which he received such deep and unalterable impressions in his maturer years. His satire, if it may be called so, is benevolent, (like the operations of the skilful and humane surgeon, who wounds only to heal,) dictated by a just regard for the honour of God, an indignant grief excited by the profligacy of the age, and a tender compassion for the souls of men.

His favourite topics are least insisted on in the piece entitled Table Talk; which therefore, with some regard to the prevailing taste, and that those, who are governed by it, may not be discouraged at the very threshold from proceeding farther, is placed first. In most of the large poems which follow, his leading design is more explicitly avowed and pursued. He aims to communicate his own perceptions of the truth, beauty, and influence of the religion of the Bible—a religion, which, however discredited by the misconduct of many, who have not renounced the Christian name, proves itself, when rightly understood, and cordially embraced, to be the grand desideratum, which alone can relieve the mind of man from painful and unavoidable anxieties, inspire it with stable peace and solid hope, and furnish those motives and prospects which, in the present state of things, are absolutely necessary to produce a conduct worthy of a rational creature, distinguished by a vastness of capacity which no assemblage of earthly good can satisfy, and by a principle and pre-intimation of immortality.

At a time when hypothesis and conjecture in philosophy are so justly exploded, and little is considered as deserving the name of knowledge, which will not stand the test of experiment, the very use of the term experimental in religious concernments is by too many unhappily rejected with disgust. But we well know, that they, who affect to despise the inward feelings which religious persons speak of, and to treat them as enthusiasm and folly, have inward feelings of their own, which, though they would, they cannot, suppress. We have been too long in the secret ourselves, to account the proud, the ambitious, or the voluptuous, happy. We must lose the remembrance of what we once were, before we can believe that a man is satisfied with himself, merely because he endeavours to appear so. A smile upon the face is often but a mask worn occasionally and in company, to prevent, if possible, a suspicion of what at the same time is passing in the heart. We know that there are people who seldom smile when they are alone, who therefore are glad to hide themselves in a throng from the violence of their own reflections; and who, while by their looks and their language they wish to persuade us they are happy, would be glad to change their conditions with a dog. But in defiance of all their efforts they continue to think, forbode, and tremble. This we know, for it has been our own state, and therefore we know how to commiserate it in others.—From this state the Bible relieved us—when we were led to read it with attention, we found ourselves described. We learned the causes of our inquietude—we were directed to a method of relief—we tried, and we were not disappointed.

Deus nobis hæc otia fecit.

We are now certain that the gospel of Christ is the power of God unto salvation to every one that believeth. It has reconciled us to God, and to ourselves, to our duty and our situation. It is the balm and cordial of the present life, and a sovereign antidote against the fear of death.

Sed hactenus hæc. Some smaller pieces upon less important subjects close the volume. Not one of them, I believe, was written with a view to publication, but I was unwilling they should be omitted.

John Newton
Charles Square, Hoxton,
February 18, 1782.

THE YEARLY DISTRESS, OR TITHING TIME AT STOCK IN ESSEX

Verses addressed to a Country Clergyman, complaining of the disagreeableness of the day annually appointed for receiving the Dues at the Parsonage.

Come, ponder well, for 'tis no jest,
To laugh it would be wrong,
The troubles of a worthy priest,
The burden of my song.

This priest he merry is and blithe
Three quarters of a year:
But oh! it cuts him like a scythe,
When tithing time draws near.

He then is full of fright and fears,
As one at point to die,
And long before the day appears,
He heaves up many a sigh.

For then the farmers come jog, jog,
Along the miry road,
Each heart as heavy as a log,
To make their payments good.

In sooth the sorrow of such days
Is not to be express'd,
When he that takes and he that pays
Are both alike distress'd.

Now all unwelcome at his gates
The clumsy swains alight,
With rueful faces and bald pates—
He trembles at the sight.

And well he may, for well he knows
Each bumpkin of the clan,
Instead of paying what he owes,
Will cheat him if he can.

So in they come—each makes his leg,
And flings his head before,
And looks as if he came to beg,
And not to quit a score.

"And how does miss and madam do,
The little boy and all?"
"All tight and well. And how do you,
Good Mr. What-d'ye-call?"

The dinner comes, and down they sit,
Were e'er such hungry folk?
There's little talking, and no wit;
It is no time to joke.

One wipes his nose upon his sleeve,
One spits upon the floor,
Yet not to give offence or grieve,
Holds up the cloth before.

The punch goes round, and they are dull
And lumpish still as ever;
Like barrels with their bellies full,
They only weigh the heavier.

At length the busy time begins.
"Come, neighbours, we must wag"—
The money chinks, down drop their chins,
Each lugging out his bag.

One talks of mildew and of frost,
And one of storms of hail,
And one of pigs that he has lost
By maggots at the tail.

Quoth one, "A rarer man than you
In pulpit none shall hear:
But yet, methinks, to tell you true,
You sell it plaguy dear."

O why are farmers made so coarse,
Or clergy made so fine?
A kick, that scarce would move a horse,
May kill a sound divine.

Then let the boobies stay at home;
'Twould cost him, I dare say,
Less trouble taking twice the sum
Without the clowns that pay.

SONNET, ADDRESSED TO HENRY COWPER, ESQ.

On his emphatical and interesting Delivery of the Defence of Warren Hastings, Esq. in the House of Lords.

Cowper, whose silver voice, task'd sometimes hard,
Legends prolix delivers in the ears

(Attentive when thou read'st) of England's peers,
Let verse at length yield thee thy just reward.

Thou wast not heard with drowsy disregard,
Expending late on all that length of plea
Thy generous powers, but silence honour'd thee,
Mute as e'er gazed on orator or bard.

Thou art not voice alone, but hast beside
Both heart and head; and couldst with music sweet
Of Attic phrase and senatorial tone,
Like thy renown'd forefathers, far and wide
Thy fame diffuse, praised not for utterance meet
Of others' speech, but magic of thy own.

LINES ADDRESSED TO DR. DARWIN, AUTHOR OF "THE BOTANIC GARDEN"

Two Poets, (poets, by report,
Not oft so well agree,)
Sweet harmonist of Flora's court!
Conspire to honour thee.

They best can judge a poet's worth,
Who oft themselves have known
The pangs of a poetic birth
By labours of their own.

We therefore pleased extol thy song,
Though various, yet complete,
Rich in embellishment as strong,
And learned as 'tis sweet.

No envy mingles with our praise,
Though, could our hearts repine
At any poet's happier lays,
They would—they must at thine.

But we, in mutual bondage knit
Of friendship's closest tie,
Can gaze on even Darwin's wit
With an unjaundiced eye;

And deem the Bard, whoe'er he be,
And howsoever known,
Who would not twine a wreath for thee,
Unworthy of his own.

ON MRS. MONTAGU'S FEATHER-HANGINGS

The birds put off their every hue
To dress a room for Montagu.
　The peacock sends his heavenly dyes,
His rainbows and his starry eyes;
The pheasant plumes, which round enfold
His mantling neck with downy gold;
The cock his arch'd tail's azure show;
And, river-blanch'd, the swan his snow.
All tribes beside of Indian name,
That glossy shine, or vivid flame,
Where rises, and where sets the day,
Whate'er they boast of rich and gay,
Contribute to the gorgeous plan,
Proud to advance it all they can.
This plumage neither dashing shower,
Nor blasts, that shake the dripping bower,
Shall drench again or discompose,
But, screen'd from every storm that blows,
It boasts a splendour ever new,
Safe with protecting Montagu.
　To the same patroness resort,
Secure of favour at her court,
Strong Genius, from whose forge of thought
Forms rise, to quick perfection wrought,
Which, though new-born, with vigour move,
Like Pallas springing arm'd from Jove—
Imagination scattering round
Wild roses over furrow'd ground,
Which Labour of his frown beguile,
And teach Philosophy a smile—
Wit flashing on Religion's side,
Whose fires, to sacred Truth applied,
The gem, though luminous before,
Obtrude on human notice more,
Like sunbeams on the golden height
Of some tall temple playing bright—
Well tutor'd Learning, from his books
Dismiss'd with grave, not haughty, looks,
Their order on his shelves exact,
Not more harmonious or compact
Than that to which he keeps confined
The various treasures of his mind—
All these to Montagu's repair,

Ambitious of a shelter there.
There Genius, Learning, Fancy, Wit,
Their ruffled plumage calm refit,
(For stormy troubles loudest roar
Around their flight who highest soar,)
And in her eye, and by her aid,
Shine safe without a fear to fade.
  She thus maintains divided sway
With yon bright regent of the day;
The Plume and Poet both we know
Their lustre to his influence owe;
And she the works of Phœbus aiding,
Both Poet saves and Plume from fading.

VERSES

Supposed to be written by Alexander Selkirk, during his solitary abode in the island of Juan Fernandez.

I am monarch of all I survey,
My right there is none to dispute;
From the centre all round to the sea
I am lord of the fowl and the brute.
O Solitude! where are the charms
That sages have seen in thy face?
Better dwell in the midst of alarms
Than reign in this horrible place.

I am out of humanity's reach,
I must finish my journey alone,
Never hear the sweet music of speech,
I start at the sound of my own.
The beasts, that roam over the plain,
My form with indifference see;
They are so unacquainted with man,
Their tameness is shocking to me.

Society, friendship, and love,
Divinely bestow'd upon man,
O, had I the wings of a dove,
How soon would I taste you again!
My sorrows I then might assuage
In the ways of religion and truth,
Might learn from the wisdom of age,
And be cheer'd by the sallies of youth.

Religion! what treasure untold

Resides in that heavenly word!
More precious than silver and gold
Or all that this earth can afford.
But the sound of the church-going bell
These valleys and rocks never heard,
Never sigh'd at the sound of a knell,
Or smiled when a sabbath appear'd.

Ye winds, that have made me your sport,
Convey to this desolate shore
Some cordial endearing report
Of a land I shall visit no more.
My friends, do they now and then send
A wish or a thought after me?
O tell me I yet have a friend,
Though a friend I am never to see.

How fleet is the glance of the mind!
Compared with the speed of its flight,
The tempest itself lags behind,
And the swift-winged arrows of light.
When I think of my own native land,
In a moment I seem to be there;
But alas! recollection at hand
Soon hurries me back to despair.

But the sea-fowl is gone to her nest,
The beast is laid down in his lair;
Even here is a season of rest,
And I to my cabin repair.
There's mercy in every place,
And mercy, encouraging thought!
Gives even affliction a grace,
And reconciles man to his lot.

ON OBSERVING SOME NAMES OF LITTLE NOTE RECORDED IN THE BIOGRAPHIA BRITANNICA

Oh, fond attempt to give a deathless lot
To names ignoble, born to be forgot!
In vain recorded in historic page,
They court the notice of a future age:
Those twinkling tiny lustres of the land
Drop one by one from Fame's neglecting hand;
Lethæan gulfs receive them as they fall,
And dark oblivion soon absorbs them all.
So when a child, as playful children use,

Has burnt to tinder a stale last year's news,
The flame extinct, he views the roving fire—
There goes my lady, and there goes the squire,
There goes the parson, oh illustrious spark!
And there, scarce less illustrious, goes the clerk!

REPORT OF AN ADJUDGED CASE, NOT TO BE FOUND IN ANY OF THE BOOKS

Between Nose and Eyes a strange contest arose,
The spectacles set them unhappily wrong;
The point in dispute was, as all the world knows,
To which the said spectacles ought to belong.

So Tongue was the lawyer, and argued the cause
With a great deal of skill, and a wig full of learning;
While chief baron Ear sat to balance the laws,
So famed for his talent in nicely discerning.

In behalf of the Nose it will quickly appear,
And your lordship, he said, will undoubtedly find,
That the Nose has had spectacles always in wear,
Which amounts to possession time out of mind.

Then holding the spectacles up to the court—
Your lordship observes they are made with a straddle,
As wide as the ridge of the Nose is; in short,
Design'd to sit close to it, just like a saddle.

Again, would your lordship a moment suppose
('Tis a case that has happen'd, and may be again)
That the visage or countenance had not a Nose,
Pray who would, or who could, wear spectacles then?

On the whole it appears, and my argument shows,
With a reasoning the court will never condemn,
That the spectacles plainly were made for the Nose,
And the Nose was as plainly intended for them.

Then shifting his side, (as a lawyer knows how,)
He pleaded again in behalf of the Eyes:
But what were his arguments few people know,
For the court did not think they were equally wise.

So his lordship decreed with a grave solemn tone,
Decisive and clear, without one if or but—
That, whenever the Nose put his spectacles on,

By daylight or candlelight—Eyes should be shut!

ON THE PROMOTION OF EDWARD THURLOW, ESQ. TO THE LORD HIGH CHANCELLORSHIP OF ENGLAND

Round Thurlow's head in early youth,
And in his sportive days,
Fair Science pour'd the light of truth,
And Genius shed his rays.

See! with united wonder cried
The experienced and the sage,
Ambition in a boy supplied
With all the skill of age!

Discernment, eloquence, and grace,
Proclaim him born to sway
The balance in the highest place,
And bear the palm away.

The praise bestow'd was just and wise;
He sprang impetuous forth,
Secure of conquest, where the prize
Attends superior worth.

So the best courser on the plain
Ere yet he starts is known,
And does but at the goal obtain
What all had deem'd his own.

ODE TO PEACE

Come, peace of mind, delightful guest!
Return, and make thy downy nest
Once more in this sad heart:
Nor riches I nor power pursue,
Nor hold forbidden joys in view;
We therefore need not part.

Where wilt thou dwell, if not with me,
From avarice and ambition free,
And pleasure's fatal wiles?
For whom, alas! dost thou prepare
The sweets that I was wont to share,

The banquet of thy smiles?

The great, the gay, shall they partake
The heaven that thou alone canst make?
And wilt thou quit the stream
That murmurs through the dewy mead,
The grove and the sequestered shed,
To be a guest with them?

For thee I panted, thee I prized,
For thee I gladly sacrificed
Whatever I loved before;
And shall I see thee start away,
And helpless, hopeless, hear thee say—
Farewell! we meet no more?

HUMAN FRAILTY

Weak and irresolute is man;
The purpose of to-day,
Woven with pains into his plan,
To-morrow rends away.

The bow well bent, and smart the spring,
Vice seems already slain;
But Passion rudely snaps the string,
And it revives again.

Some foe to his upright intent
Finds out his weaker part;
Virtue engages his assent,
But Pleasure wins his heart.

'Tis here the folly of the wise
Through all his art we view;
And, while his tongue the charge denies,
His conscience owns it true.

Bound on a voyage of awful length
And dangers little known,
A stranger to superior strength,
Man vainly trusts his own.

But oars alone can ne'er prevail
To reach the distant coast;
The breath of Heaven must swell the sail,

Or all the toil is lost.

THE MODERN PATRIOT

Rebellion is my theme all day;
I only wish 'twould come
(As who knows but perhaps it may?)
A little nearer home.

Yon roaring boys, who rave and fight
On t'other side the Atlantic,
I always held them in the right,
But most so when most frantic.

When lawless mobs insult the court,
That man shall be my toast,
If breaking windows be the sport,
Who bravely breaks the most.

But O! for him my fancy culls
The choicest flowers she bears,
Who constitutionally pulls
Your house about your ears.

Such civil broils are my delight,
Though some folks can't endure them,
Who say the mob are mad outright,
And that a rope must cure them.

A rope! I wish we patriots had
Such strings for all who need 'em—
What! hang a man for going mad!
Then farewell British freedom.

ON THE BURNING OF LORD MANSFIELD'S LIBRARY, TOGETHER WITH HIS MSS. BY THE MOB, IN THE MONTH OF JUNE, 1780

So then—the Vandals of our isle,
Sworn foes to sense and law,
Have burnt to dust a nobler pile
Than ever Roman saw!

And Murray sighs o'er Pope and Swift,
And many a treasure more,

The well-judged purchase, and the gift
That graced his letter'd store.

Their pages mangled, burnt, and torn,
The loss was his alone;
But ages yet to come shall mourn
The burning of his own.

ON THE SAME

When wit and genius meet their doom
In all devouring flame,
They tell us of the fate of Rome,
And bid us fear the same.

O'er Murray's loss the muses wept,
They felt the rude alarm,
Yet bless'd the guardian care that kept
His sacred head from harm.

There Memory, like the bee that's fed
From Flora's balmy store,
The quintessence of all he read
Had treasured up before.

The lawless herd, with fury blind,
Have done him cruel wrong;
The flowers are gone—but still we find
The honey on his tongue.

THE LOVE OF THE WORLD REPROVED; OR, HYPOCRISY DETECTED

Thus says the prophet of the Turk,
Good Mussulman, abstain from pork;
There is a part in every swine
No friend or follower of mine
May taste, whate'er his inclination,
On pain of excommunication.
Such Mahomet's mysterious charge,
And thus he left the point at large.
Had he the sinful part express'd,
They might with safety eat the rest;
But for one piece they thought it hard
From the whole hog to be debarr'd;

And set their wit at work to find
What joint the prophet had in mind.
Much controversy straight arose,
These choose the back, the belly those;
By some 'tis confidently said
He meant not to forbid the head;
While others at that doctrine rail,
And piously prefer the tail.
Thus, conscience freed from every clog,
Mahometans eat up the hog.
  You laugh—'tis well—the tale applied
May make you laugh on t'other side.
Renounce the world—the preacher cries.
We do—a multitude replies.
While one as innocent regards
A snug and friendly game at cards;
And one, whatever you may say,
Can see no evil in a play;
Some love a concert, or a race;
And others shooting, and the chase.
Reviled and loved, renounced and follow'd,
Thus, bit by bit, the world is swallow'd;
Each thinks his neighbour makes too free,
Yet likes a slice as well as he:
With sophistry their sauce they sweeten,
Till quite from tail to snout 'tis eaten.

ON THE DEATH OF MRS. (NOW LADY) THROCKMORTON'S BULLFINCH

Ye nymphs! if e'er your eyes were red
With tears o'er hapless favourites shed,
O share Maria's grief!
Her favourite, even in his cage,
(What will not hunger's cruel rage?)
Assassin'd by a thief.

Where Rhenus strays his vines among,
The egg was laid from which he sprung;
And, though by nature mute,
Or only with a whistle blest,
Well taught he all the sounds express'd
Of flageolet or flute.

The honours of his ebon poll
Were brighter than the sleekest mole,
His bosom of the hue

With which Aurora decks the skies,
When piping winds shall soon arise,
To sweep away the dew.

Above, below, in all the house,
Dire foe alike of bird and mouse
No cat had leave to dwell;
And Bully's cage supported stood
On props of smoothest shaven wood,
Large-built and latticed well.

Well latticed—but the grate, alas!
Not rough with wire of steel or brass,
For Bully's plumage sake,
But smooth with wands from Ouse's side,
With which, when neatly peel'd and dried,
The swains their baskets make.

Night veil'd the pole: all seem'd secure:
When, led by instinct sharp and sure,
Subsistence to provide,
A beast forth sallied on the scout,
Long back'd, long tail'd, with whisker'd snout,
And badger-colour'd hide.

He, entering at the study door,
Its ample area 'gan explore;
And something in the wind
Conjectured, sniffing round and round,
Better than all the books he found,
Food chiefly for the mind.

Just then, by adverse fate impress'd,
A dream disturb'd poor Bully's rest;
In sleep he seem'd to view
A rat fast clinging to the cage,
And, screaming at the sad presage,
Awoke and found it true.

For, aided both by ear and scent,
Right to his mark the monster went—
Ah, muse! forbear to speak
Minute the horrors that ensued;
His teeth were strong, the cage was wood—
He left poor Bully's beak.

O had he made that too his prey;
That beak, whence issued many a lay

Of such mellifluous tone,
Might have repaid him well, I wote,
For silencing so sweet a throat,
Fast stuck within his own.

Maria weeps—the Muses mourn—
So when, by Bacchanalians torn,
On Thracian Hebrus' side
The tree-enchanter Orpheus fell,
His head alone remain'd to tell
The cruel death he died.

THE ROSE

The rose had been wash'd, just wash'd in a shower,
Which Mary to Anna convey'd,
The plentiful moisture encumber'd the flower,
And weigh'd down its beautiful head.

The cup was all fill'd, and the leaves were all wet,
And it seem'd, to a fanciful view,
To weep for the buds it had left, with regret,
On the flourishing bush where it grew.

I hastily seized it, unfit as it was
For a nosegay, so dripping and drown'd,
And swinging it rudely, too rudely, alas!
I snapp'd it, it fell to the ground.

And such, I exclaim'd, is the pitiless part
Some act by the delicate mind,
Regardless of wringing and breaking a heart
Already to sorrow resign'd.

This elegant rose, had I shaken it less,
Might have bloom'd with its owner a while;
And the tear, that is wiped with a little address,
May be follow'd perhaps by a smile.

THE DOVES

Reasoning at every step he treads,
Man yet mistakes his way
While meaner things, whom instinct leads,

Are rarely known to stray.

One silent eve I wander'd late,
And heard the voice of love;
The turtle thus address'd her mate,
And soothed the listening dove:

Our mutual bond of faith and truth
No time shall disengage,
Those blessings of our early youth
Shall cheer our latest age:

While innocence without disguise,
And constancy sincere,
Shall fill the circles of those eyes,
And mine can read them there;

Those ills, that wait on all below,
Shall ne'er be felt by me,
Or gently felt, and only so,
As being shared with thee.

When lightnings flash among the trees,
Or kites are hovering near,
I fear lest thee alone they seize,
And know no other fear.

'Tis then I feel myself a wife,
And press thy wedded side,
Resolved a union form'd for life
Death never shall divide.

But oh! if, fickle and unchaste,
(Forgive a transient thought,)
Thou couldst become unkind at last,
And scorn thy present lot,

No need of lightnings from on high,
Or kites with cruel beak;
Denied the endearments of thine eye,
This widow'd heart would break.

Thus sang the sweet sequester'd bird,
Soft as the passing wind,
And I recorded what I heard,
A lesson for mankind.

A FABLE

A raven, while with glossy breast
Her new-laid eggs she fondly press'd,
And, on her wicker-work high mounted,
Her chickens prematurely counted,
(A fault philosophers might blame,
If quite exempted from the same,)
Enjoy'd at ease the genial day;
'Twas April, as the bumpkins say,
The legislature call'd it May.
But suddenly a wind, as high
As ever swept a winter sky,
Shook the young leaves about her ears,
And fill'd her with a thousand fears,
Lest the rude blast should snap the bough,
And spread her golden hopes below.
But just at eve the blowing weather
And all her fears were hush'd together:
And now, quoth poor unthinking Ralph,
'Tis over, and the brood is safe;
(For ravens, though, as birds of omen,
They teach both conjurors and old women
To tell us what is to befall,
Can't prophesy themselves at all.)
The morning came, when neighbour Hodge,
Who long had mark'd her airy lodge,
And destined all the treasure there
A gift to his expecting fair,
Climb'd like a squirrel to his dray,
And bore the worthless prize away.

MORAL

'Tis Providence alone secures
In every change both mine and yours:
Safety consists not in escape
From dangers of a frightful shape;
An earthquake may be bid to spare
The man that's strangled by a hair.
Fate steals along with silent tread,
Found oft'nest in what least we dread,
Frowns in the storm with angry brow,
But in the sunshine strikes the blow.

ODE TO APOLLO. ON AN INKGLASS ALMOST DRIED IN THE SUN

Patron of all those luckless brains,
That, to the wrong side leaning,
Indite much metre with much pains,
And little or no meaning;

Ah why, since oceans, rivers, streams,
That water all the nations,
Pay tribute to thy glorious beams,
In constant exhalations;

Why, stooping from the noon of day,
Too covetous of drink,
Apollo, hast thou stolen away
A poet's drop of ink?

Upborne into the viewless air,
It floats a vapour now,
Impell'd through regions dense and rare,
By all the winds that blow.

Ordain'd perhaps, ere summer flies,
Combined with millions more,
To form an iris in the skies,
Though black and foul before.

Illustrious drop! and happy then
Beyond the happiest lot,
Of all that ever pass'd my pen,

So soon to be forgot!
Phœbus, if such be thy design.
To place it in thy bow,
Give wit, that what is left may shine
With equal grace below.

A COMPARISON

The lapse of time and rivers is the same,
Both speed their journey with a restless stream,
The silent pace, with which they steal away,
No wealth can bribe, no prayers persuade to stay;
Alike irrevocable both when past,

And a wide ocean swallows both at last.
Though each resemble each in every part,
A difference strikes at length the musing heart;
Streams never flow in vain; where streams abound,
How laughs the land with various plenty crown'd!
But time, that should enrich the nobler mind,
Neglected leaves a dreary waste behind.

ANOTHER. ADDRESSED TO A YOUNG LADY

Sweet stream that winds through yonder glade,
Apt emblem of a virtuous maid—
Silent and chaste she steals along,
Far from the world's gay busy throng;
With gentle yet prevailing force,
Intent upon her destined course;
Graceful and useful all she does,
Blessing and blest where'er she goes.
Pure-bosom'd as that watery glass,
And heaven reflected in her face.

THE POET'S NEW YEAR'S GIFT. TO MRS. (NOW LADY) THROCKMORTON

Maria! I have every good
For thee wish'd many a time,
Both sad, and in a cheerful mood,
But never yet in rhyme.

To wish thee fairer is no need,
More prudent, or more sprightly,
Or more ingenious, or more freed
From temper-flaws unsightly.

What favour then not yet possess'd
Can I for thee require,
In wedded love already blest,
To thy whole heart's desire?

None here is happy but in part:
Full bliss is bliss divine;
There dwells some wish in every heart,
And doubtless one in thine.

That wish on some fair future day,

Which fate shall brightly gild,
('Tis blameless, be it what it may,)
I wish it all fulfill'd.

PAIRING TIME ANTICIPATED. A FABLE

I shall not ask Jean Jaques Rousseau
If birds confabulate or no;
'Tis clear, that they were always able
To hold discourse, at least in fable;
And e'en the child who knows no better
Than to interpret, by the letter,
A story of a cock and bull,
Must have a most uncommon skull.
　It chanced then on a winter's day,
But warm, and bright, and calm as May,
The birds, conceiving a design
To forestall sweet St. Valentine,
In many an orchard, copse, and grove,
Assembled on affairs of love,
And with much twitter and much chatter
Began to agitate the matter.
At length a Bullfinch, who could boast
More years and wisdom than the most,
Entreated, opening wide his beak,
A moment's liberty to speak;
And, silence publicly enjoin'd,
Deliver'd briefly thus his mind:
　My friends! be cautious how ye treat
The subject upon which we meet;
I fear we shall have winter yet.
　A Finch, whose tongue knew no control,
With golden wing and satin poll,
A last year's bird, who ne'er had tried
What marriage means, thus pert replied:
　Methinks the gentleman, quoth she,
Opposite in the apple tree,
By his good will would keep us single
Till yonder heaven and earth shall mingle,
Or (which is likelier to befall)
Till death exterminate us all.
I marry without more ado,
My dear Dick Redcap, what say you?
　Dick heard, and tweedling, ogling, bridling,
Turning short round, strutting and sideling,
Attested, glad, his approbation

Of an immediate conjugation.
Their sentiments so well express'd
Influenced mightily the rest,
All pair'd, and each pair built a nest.
   But, though the birds were thus in haste,
The leaves came on not quite so fast,
And destiny, that sometimes bears
An aspect stern on man's affairs,
Not altogether smiled on theirs.
The wind, of late breathed gently forth,
Now shifted east, and east by north;
Bare trees and shrubs but ill, you know,
Could shelter them from rain or snow,
Stepping into their nests, they paddled,
Themselves were chill'd, their eggs were addled;
Soon every father bird and mother
Grew quarrelsome, and peck'd each other,
Parted without the least regret,
Except that they had ever met,
And learn'd in future to be wiser,
Than to neglect a good adviser.

MORAL

Misses! the tale that I relate
This lesson seems to carry—
Choose not alone a proper mate,
But proper time to marry.

THE DOG AND THE WATER LILY. NO FABLE

The noon was shady, and soft airs
Swept Ouse's silent tide,
When, 'scaped from literary cares,
I wander'd on his side.

My spaniel, prettiest of his race,
And high in pedigree,
(Two nymphs adorn'd with every grace
That spaniel found for me,)

Now wanton'd lost in flags and reeds,
Now starting into sight,
Pursued the swallow o'er the meads
With scarce a slower flight.

It was the time when Ouse display'd
His lilies newly blown;
Their beauties I intent survey'd,
And one I wish'd my own.

With cane extended far I sought
To steer it close to land;
But still the prize, though nearly caught,
Escaped my eager hand.

Beau mark'd my unsuccessful pains
With fix'd considerate face,
And puzzling set his puppy brains
To comprehend the case.

But with a cherup clear and strong
Dispersing all his dream,
I thence withdrew, and follow'd long
The windings of the stream.

My ramble ended, I return'd;
Beau, trotting far before,
The floating wreath again discern'd,
And plunging, left the shore.

I saw him with that lily cropp'd
Impatient swim to meet
My quick approach, and soon he dropp'd
The treasure at my feet.

Charm'd with the sight, the world, I cried,
Shall hear of this thy deed:
My dog shall mortify the pride
Of man's superior breed:

But chief myself I will enjoin,
Awake at duty's call,
To show a love as prompt as thine
To Him who gives me all.

THE WINTER NOSEGAY

What Nature, alas! has denied
To the delicate growth of our isle,
Art has in a measure supplied,
And winter is deck'd with a smile.

See, Mary, what beauties I bring
From the shelter of that sunny shed,
Where the flowers have the charms of the spring,
Though abroad they are frozen and dead.

'Tis a bower of Arcadian sweets,
Where Flora is still in her prime,
A fortress to which she retreats
From the cruel assaults of the clime.
While earth wears a mantle of snow,
These pinks are as fresh and as gay
As the fairest and sweetest that blow
On the beautiful bosom of May.

See how they have safely survived
The frowns of a sky so severe;
Such Mary's true love, that has lived
Through many a turbulent year.
The charms of the late-blowing rose
Seem graced with a livelier hue,
And the winter of sorrow best shows
The truth of a friend such as you.

THE POET, THE OYSTER, AND SENSITIVE PLANT

An Oyster, cast upon the shore,
Was heard, though never heard before,
Complaining in a speech well worded,
And worthy thus to be recorded:—
    Ah, hapless wretch! condemn'd to dwell
For ever in my native shell;
Ordain'd to move when others please,
Not for my own content or ease;
But toss'd and buffeted about,
Now in the water and now out.
'Twere better to be born a stone,
Of ruder shape, and feeling none,
Than with a tenderness like mine,
And sensibilities so fine!
I envy that unfeeling shrub,
Fast rooted against every rub.
The plant he meant grew not far off,
And felt the sneer with scorn enough:
Was hurt, disgusted, mortified,
And with asperity replied:
    (When, cry the botanists, and stare,

Did plants call'd sensitive grow there?
No matter when—a poet's muse is
To make them grow just where she chooses)
   You shapeless nothing in a dish,
You that are but almost a fish,
I scorn your coarse insinuation,
And have most plentiful occasion
To wish myself the rock I view,
Or such another dolt as you:
For many a grave and learned clerk
And many a gay unletter'd spark,
With curious touch examines me,
If I can feel as well as he;
And when I bend, retire, and shrink,
Says—Well, tis more than one would think!
Thus life is spent (oh fie upon't)
In being touch'd, and crying—Don't!
   A poet, in his evening walk,
O'erheard and check'd this idle talk.
And your fine sense, he said, and yours,
Whatever evil it endures,
Deserves not, if so soon offended,
Much to be pitied or commended.
Disputes, though short, are far too long,
Where both alike are in the wrong;
Your feelings in their full amount
Are all upon your own account.
   You, in your grotto-work enclosed,
Complain of being thus exposed;
Yet nothing feel in that rough coat
Save when the knife is at your throat,
Wherever driven by wind or tide,
Exempt from every ill beside.
   And as for you, my Lady Squeamish,
Who reckon every touch a blemish,
If all the plants, that can be found
Embellishing the scene around,
Should droop and wither where they grow,
You would not feel at all—not you.
The noblest minds their virtue prove
By pity, sympathy, and love:
These, these are feelings truly fine,
And prove their owner half divine.
   His censure reach'd them as he dealt it
And each by shrinking show'd he felt it.

THE SHRUBBERY. WRITTEN IN A TIME OF AFFLICTION

Oh, happy shades—to me unblest!
Friendly to peace, but not to me!
How ill the scene that offers rest,
And heart that cannot rest, agree!

This glassy stream, that spreading pine,
Those alders, quivering to the breeze,
Might soothe a soul less hurt than mine,
And please, if any thing could please.

But fix'd unalterable Care
Foregoes not what she feels within,
Shows the same sadness every where,
And slights the season and the scene.

For all that pleased in wood or lawn,
While Peace possess'd these silent bowers,
Her animating smile withdrawn,
Has lost its beauties and its powers.

The saint or moralist should tread
This moss-grown alley musing, slow;
They seek like me the secret shade,
But not like me to nourish woe!

Me fruitful scenes and prospects waste
Alike admonish not to roam;
These tell me of enjoyments past,
And those of sorrows yet to come.

MUTUAL FORBEARANCE. NECESSARY TO THE HAPPINESS OF THE MARRIED STATE

The lady thus address'd her spouse—
What a mere dungeon is this house!
By no means large enough; and was it,
Yet this dull room, and that dark closet,
Those hangings with their worn-out graces,
Long beards, long noses, and pale faces,
Are such an antiquated scene,
They overwhelm me with the spleen.
Sir Humphrey, shooting in the dark,
Makes answer quite beside the mark:
No doubt, my dear, I bade him come,
Engaged myself to be at home,

And shall expect him at the door
Precisely when the clock strikes four.
   You are so deaf, the lady cried,
(And raised her voice, and frown'd beside,)
You are so sadly deaf, my dear,
What shall I do to make you hear?
   Dismiss poor Harry! he replies;
Some people are more nice than wise:
For one slight trespass all this stir?
What if he did ride whip and spur,
'Twas but a mile—your favourite horse
Will never look one hair the worse.
   Well, I protest 'tis past all bearing—
Child! I am rather hard of hearing—
Yes, truly—one must scream and bawl:
I tell you, you can't hear at all!
Then, with a voice exceeding low,
No matter if you hear or no.
   Alas! and is domestic strife,
That sorest ill of human life,
A plague so little to be fear'd,
As to be wantonly incurr'd,
To gratify a fretful passion,
On every trivial provocation?
The kindest and the happiest pair
Will find occasion to forbear;
And something every day they live
To pity, and perhaps forgive.
But if infirmities, that fall
In common to the lot of all,
A blemish or a sense impair'd,
Are crimes so little to be spared,
Then farewell all that must create
The comfort of the wedded state;
Instead of harmony, 'tis jar,
And tumult, and intestine war.
   The love that cheers life's latest stage,
Proof against sickness and old age,
Preserved by virtue from declension,
Becomes not weary of attention;
But lives, when that exterior grace,
Which first inspired the flame, decays.
'Tis gentle, delicate, and kind,
To faults compassionate or blind,
And will with sympathy endure
Those evils it would gladly cure:
But angry, coarse, and harsh expression,
Shows love to be a mere profession;

Proves that the heart is none of his,
Or soon expels him if it is.

THE NEGRO'S COMPLAINT

Forced from home and all its pleasures,
Afric's coast I left forlorn;
To increase a stranger's treasures,
O'er the raging billows borne.
Men from England bought and sold me,
Paid my price in paltry gold;
But, though slave they have enroll'd me,
Minds are never to be sold.

Still in thought as free as ever,
What are England's rights, I ask,
Me from my delights to sever,
Me to torture, me to task?
Fleecy locks and black complexion
Cannot forfeit nature's claim;
Skins may differ, but affection
Dwells in white and black the same.

Why did all-creating Nature
Make the plant for which we toil?
Sighs must fan it, tears must water,
Sweat of ours must dress the soil.
Think, ye masters iron-hearted,
Lolling at your jovial boards,
Think how many backs have smarted
For the sweets your cane affords.

Is there, as ye sometimes tell us,
Is there One who reigns on high?
Has he bid you buy and sell us,
Speaking from his throne, the sky?
Ask him, if your knotted scourges,
Matches, blood-extorting screws,
Are the means that duty urges
Agents of his will to use?

Hark! he answers—wild tornadoes,
Strewing yonder sea with wrecks;
Wasting towns, plantations, meadows,
Are the voice with which he speaks.
He, foreseeing what vexations

Afric's sons should undergo,
Fix'd their tyrants' habitations
Where his whirlwinds answer—no.

By our blood in Afric wasted,
Ere our necks received the chain;
By the miseries that we tasted,
Crossing in your barks the main;
By our sufferings, since ye brought us
To the man-degrading mart,
All sustain'd by patience, taught us
Only by a broken heart;

Deem our nation brutes no longer,
Till some reason ye shall find
Worthier of regard, and stronger
Than the colour of our kind.
Slaves of gold, whose sordid dealings
Tarnish all your boasted powers,
Prove that you have human feelings,
Ere you proudly question ours!

PITY FOR POOR AFRICANS

Video meliora proboque,
Deteriora sequor.

I own I am shock'd at the purchase of slaves,
And fear those who buy them and sell them are knaves;
What I hear of their hardships, their tortures, and groans,
Is almost enough to draw pity from stones.

I pity them greatly, but I must be mum,
For how could we do without sugar and rum?
Especially sugar, so needful we see?
What, give up our desserts, our coffee, and tea!

Besides, if we do, the French, Dutch, and Danes
Will heartily thank us, no doubt, for our pains;
If we do not buy the poor creatures, they will,
And tortures and groans will be multiplied still.

If foreigners likewise would give up the trade,
Much more in behalf of your wish might be said;
But, while they get riches by purchasing blacks,
Pray tell me why we may not also go snacks?

Your scruples and arguments bring to my mind
A story so pat, you may think it is coin'd,
On purpose to answer you, out of my mint;
But I can assure you I saw it in print.

A youngster at school, more sedate than the rest,
Had once his integrity put to the test;
His comrades had plotted an orchard to rob,
And ask'd him to go and assist in the job.

He was shock'd, sir, like you, and answer'd, "Oh no!
What! rob our good neighbour! I pray you don't go;
Besides, the man's poor, his orchard's his bread,
Then think of his children, for they must be fed."

"You speak very fine, and you look very grave,
But apples we want, and apples we'll have;
If you will go with us, you shall have a share,
If not, you shall have neither apple nor pear."

They spoke, and Tom pondered—"I see they will go;
Poor man! what a pity to injure him so!
Poor man! I would save him his fruit if I could,
But staying behind will do him no good.

"If the matter depended alone upon me,
His apples might hang till they dropp'd from the tree;
But, since they will take them, I think I'll go too,
He will lose none by me, though I get a few."

His scruples thus silenced, Tom felt more at ease,
And went with his comrades the apples to seize;
He blamed and protested, but join'd in the plan:
He shared in the plunder, but pitied the man.

THE MORNING DREAM

'Twas in the glad season of spring,
Asleep at the dawn of the day,
I dream'd what I cannot but sing,
So pleasant it seem'd as I lay.
I dream'd that, on ocean afloat,
Far hence to the westward I sail'd,
While the billows high lifted the boat,
And the fresh-blowing breeze never fail'd.

In the steerage a woman I saw,
Such at least was the form that she wore,
Whose beauty impress'd me with awe,
Ne'er taught me by woman before.
She sat, and a shield at her side
Shed light, like a sun on the waves,
And smiling divinely, she cried—
"I go to make freemen of slaves."

Then, raising her voice to a strain
The sweetest that ear ever heard,
She sung of the slave's broken chain,
Wherever her glory appear'd.
Some clouds, which had over us hung,
Fled, chased by her melody clear,
And methought while she liberty sung,
'Twas liberty only to hear.

Thus swiftly dividing the flood,
To a slave-cultured island we came,
Where a demon, her enemy, stood—
Oppression his terrible name.
In his hand, as the sign of his sway,
A scourge hung with lashes he bore,
And stood looking out for his prey
From Africa's sorrowful shore.

But soon as, approaching the land,
That goddesslike woman he view'd,
The scourge he let fall from his hand,
With blood of his subjects imbrued.
I saw him both sicken and die,
And, the moment the monster expired,
Heard shouts, that ascended the sky,
From thousands with rapture inspired.

Awaking, how could I but muse
At what such a dream should betide?
But soon my ear caught the glad news,
Which served my weak thought for a guide;
That Britannia, renown'd o'er the waves
For the hatred she ever has shown
To the black-sceptred rulers of slaves,
Resolves to have none of her own.

THE DIVERTING HISTORY OF JOHN GILPIN;

SHOWING HOW HE WENT FARTHER THAN HE INTENDED, AND CAME SAFE HOME AGAIN

John Gilpin was a citizen
Of credit and renown,
A trainband captain eke was he
Of famous London town.

John Gilpin's spouse said to her dear:
Though wedded we have been
These twice ten tedious years, yet we
No holiday have seen.

To-morrow is our wedding-day,
And we will then repair
Unto the Bell at Edmonton
All in a chaise and pair.

My sister, and my sister's child,
Myself, and children three,
Will fill the chaise; so you must ride
On horseback after we.

He soon replied, I do admire
Of womankind but one,
And you are she, my dearest dear,
Therefore it shall be done.

I am a linendraper bold,
As all the world doth know,
And my good friend the calendrer
Will lend his horse to go.

Quoth Mrs. Gilpin, That's well said;
And for that wine is dear,
We will be furnish'd with our own,
Which is both bright and clear.

John Gilpin kiss'd his loving wife;
O'erjoyed was he to find,
That, though on pleasure she was bent,
She had a frugal mind.

The morning came, the chaise was brought,
But yet was not allow'd
To drive up to the door, lest all
Should say that she was proud.

So three doors off the chaise was stay'd,
Where they did all get in;
Six precious souls, and all agog
To dash through thick and thin.

Smack went the whip, round went the wheels,
Were never folk so glad,
The stones did rattle underneath,
As if Cheapside were mad.

John Gilpin at his horse's side
Seized fast the flowing mane,
And up he got, in haste to ride,
But soon came down again;

For saddletree scarce reach'd had he,
His journey to begin,
When, turning round his head, he saw
Three customers come in.

So down he came; for loss of time,
Although it grieved him sore,
Yet loss of pence, full well he knew,
Would trouble him much more.

'Twas long before the customers
Were suited to their mind,
When Betty screaming came down stairs,
"The wine is left behind!"

Good lack! quoth he—yet bring it me,
My leathern belt likewise,
In which I bear my trusty sword
When I do exercise.

Now mistress Gilpin (careful soul!)
Had two stone bottles found,
To hold the liquor that she loved,
And keep it safe and sound.

Each bottle had a curling ear,
Through which the belt he drew,
And hung a bottle on each side,
To make his balance true.

Then over all, that he might be
Equipp'd from top to toe,

His long red cloak, well brush'd and neat,
He manfully did throw.

Now see him mounted once again
Upon his nimble steed,
Full slowly pacing o'er the stones,
With caution and good heed.

But finding soon a smoother road
Beneath his well shod feet,
The snorting beast began to trot,
Which gall'd him in his seat.

So, fair and softly, John he cried,
But John he cried in vain;
That trot became a gallop soon,
In spite of curb and rein.

So stooping down, as needs he must
Who cannot sit upright,
He grasp'd the mane with both his hands,
And eke with all his might.

His horse, who never in that sort
Had handled been before,
What thing upon his back had got
Did wonder more and more.

Away went Gilpin, neck or nought;
Away went hat and wig;
He little dreamt, when he set out,
Of running such a rig.

The wind did blow, the cloak did fly,
Like streamer long and gay,
Till, loop and button failing both,
At last it flew away.

Then might all people well discern
The bottles he had slung;
A bottle swinging at each side,
As hath been said or sung.

The dogs did bark, the children scream'd
Up flew the windows all;
And every soul cried out, Well done!
As loud as he could bawl.

Away went Gilpin—who but he?
His fame soon spread around,
He carries weight! he rides a race!
'Tis for a thousand pound!

And still, as fast as he drew near,
'Twas wonderful to view,
How in a trice the turnpike men
Their gates wide open threw.

And now, as he went bowing down
His reeking head full low,
The bottles twain behind his back
Were shatter'd at a blow.

Down ran the wine into the road,
Most piteous to be seen,
Which made his horse's flanks to smoke,
As they had basted been.

But still he seem'd to carry weight,
With leathern girdle braced;
For all might see the bottle necks
Still dangling at his waist.

Thus all through merry Islington
These gambols he did play,
Until he came unto the Wash
Of Edmonton so gay;

And there he threw the wash about
On both sides of the way,
Just like unto a trundling mop,
Or a wild goose at play.

At Edmonton, his loving wife
From the balcony spied
Her tender husband, wondering much
To see how he did ride.

Stop, stop, John Gilpin!—Here's the house!
They all at once did cry;
The dinner waits, and we are tired:
Said Gilpin—So am I!

But yet his horse was not a whit
Inclined to tarry there;
For why?—his owner had a house

Full ten miles off, at Ware.

So like an arrow swift he flew,
Shot by an archer strong;
So did he fly—which brings me to
The middle of my song.

Away went Gilpin out of breath,
And sore against his will,
Till at his friend the calendrer's
His horse at last stood still.

The calendrer, amazed to see
His neighbour in such trim,
Laid down his pipe, flew to the gate,
And thus accosted him:

What news? what news? your tidings tell;
Tell me you must and shall—
Say why bareheaded you are come,
Or why you come at all?

Now Gilpin had a pleasant wit,
And loved a timely joke!
And thus unto the calendrer
In merry guise he spoke:

I came because your horse would come,
And, if I well forebode,
My hat and wig will soon be here,
They are upon the road.

The calendrer, right glad to find
His friend in merry pin,
Return'd him not a single word,
But to the house went in;

Whence straight he came with hat and wig;
A wig that flow'd behind,
A hat not much the worse for wear,
Each comely in its kind.

He held them up, and in his turn
Thus show'd his ready wit:
My head is twice as big as yours,
They therefore needs must fit.

But let me scrape the dirt away

That hangs upon your face;
And stop and eat, for well you may
Be in a hungry case.

Said John, It is my wedding-day,
And all the world would stare,
If wife should dine at Edmonton,
And I should dine at Ware.

So turning to his horse, he said,
I am in haste to dine;
'Twas for your pleasure you came here,
You shall go back for mine.

Ah luckless speech, and bootless boast!
For which he paid full dear;
For, while he spake, a braying ass
Did sing most loud and clear;

Whereat his horse did snort, as he
Had heard a lion roar,
And gallop'd off with all his might,
As he had done before.

Away went Gilpin, and away,
Went Gilpin's hat and wig:
He lost them sooner than at first,
For why?—they were too big.

Now mistress Gilpin, when she saw
Her husband posting down
Into the country far away,
She pull'd out half-a-crown;

And thus unto the youth she said,
That drove them to the Bell,
This shall be yours, when you bring back
My husband safe and well.

The youth did ride, and soon did meet
John coming back amain;
Whom in a trice he tried to stop,
By catching at his rein;

But, not performing what he meant,
And gladly would have done,
The frighted steed he frighted more,
And made him faster run.

Away went Gilpin, and away
Went postboy at his heels,
The postboy's horse right glad to miss
The lumbering of the wheels.

Six gentlemen upon the road
Thus seeing Gilpin fly,
With postboy scampering in the rear,
They raised the hue and cry:—

Stop thief! stop thief!—a highwayman!
Not one of them was mute;
And all and each that pass'd that way
Did join in the pursuit.

And now the turnpike gates again
Flew open in short space;
The toll-men thinking as before,
That Gilpin rode a race.

And so he did, and won it too,
For he got first to town;
Nor stopp'd till where he had got up
He did again get down.

Now let us sing, long live the king,
And Gilpin long live he;
And when he next doth ride abroad,
May I be there to see!

THE NIGHTINGALE AND GLOWWORM

A Nightingale, that all day long
Had cheer'd the village with his song,
Nor yet at eve his note suspended,
Nor yet when eventide was ended,
Began to feel, as well he might,
The keen demands of appetite;
When, looking eagerly around
He spied far off, upon the ground,
A something shining in the dark,
And knew the glowworm by his spark;
So stooping down from hawthorn top,
He thought to put him in his crop.
The worm, aware of his intent,

Harangued him thus, right eloquent—
   Did you admire my lamp, quoth he,
As much as I your minstrelsy,
You would abhor to do me wrong
As much as I to spoil your song;
For 'twas the self-same Power divine
Taught you to sing, and me to shine;
That you with music, I with light,
Might beautify and cheer the night.
The songster heard his short oration.
And, warbling out his approbation,
Released him, as my story tells,
And found a supper somewhere else.
   Hence jarring sectaries may learn
Their real interest to discern;
That brother should not war with brother,
And worry and devour each other;
But sing and shine by sweet consent,
Till life's poor transient night is spent,
Respecting in each other's case
The gifts of nature and of grace.
   Those Christians best deserve the name
Who studiously make peace their aim;
Peace both the duty and the prize
Of him that creeps and him that flies.

AN EPISTLE TO AN AFFLICTED PROTESTANT LADY IN FRANCE

Madam,
A stranger's purpose in these lays
Is to congratulate, and not to praise.
To give the creature the Creator's due
Were sin in me, and an offence to you.
From man to man, or e'en to woman paid,
Praise is the medium of a knavish trade,
A coin by craft for folly's use design'd,
Spurious, and only current with the blind.
   The path of sorrow, and that path alone,
Leads to the land where sorrow is unknown;
No traveller ever reach'd that blest abode,
Who found not thorns and briers in his road.
The world may dance along the flowery plain,
Cheer'd as they go by many a sprightly strain,
Where Nature has her mossy velvet spread,
With unshod feet they yet securely tread,
Admonish'd, scorn the caution and the friend,

Bent all on pleasure, heedless of its end.
But He, who knew what human hearts would prove,
How slow to learn the dictates of his love,
That, hard by nature and of stubborn will,
A life of ease would make them harder still,
In pity to the souls his grace design'd
To rescue from the ruins of mankind,
Call'd for a cloud to darken all their years,
And said, "Go, spend them in the vale of tears."
O balmy gales of soul-reviving air!
O salutary streams, that murmur there!
These flowing from the fount of grace above,
Those breathed from lips of everlasting love.
The flinty soil indeed their feet annoys;
Chill blasts of trouble nip their springing joys;
An envious world will interpose its frown,
To mar delights superior to its own;
And many a pang, experienced still within,
Reminds them of their hated inmate, Sin:
But ills of every shape and every name,
Transform'd to blessings, miss their cruel aim:
And every moment's calm, that soothes the breast,
Is given in earnest of eternal rest.
   Ah, be not sad, although thy lot be cast
Far from the flock, and in a boundless waste!
No shepherd's tents within thy view appear,
But the chief Shepherd even there is near;
Thy tender sorrows and thy plaintive strain
Flow in a foreign land, but not in vain;
Thy tears all issue from a source divine,
And every drop bespeaks a Saviour thine—
So once in Gideon's fleece the dews were found,
And drought on all the drooping herbs around.

TO THE REV. W. CAWTHORNE UNWIN

Unwin, I should but ill repay
The kindness of a friend,
Whose worth deserves as warm a lay
As ever friendship penn'd,
Thy name omitted in a page
That would reclaim a vicious age.

A union form'd, as mine with thee,
Not rashly, or in sport,
May be as fervent in degree

And faithful in its sort,
And may as rich in comfort prove,
As that of true fraternal love.

The bud inserted in the rind,
The bud of peach or rose,
Adorns, though differing in its kind,
The stock whereon it grows,
With flower as sweet, or fruit as fair,
As if produced by nature there.

Not rich, I render what I may,
I seize thy name in haste,
And place it in this first essay,
Lest this should prove the last.
'Tis where it should be—in a plan
That holds in view the good of man.

The poet's lyre, to fix his fame,
Should be the poet's heart;
Affection lights a brighter flame
Than ever blazed by art.
No muses on these lines attend,
I sink the poet in the friend.

TO THE REVEREND MR. NEWTON AN INVITATION INTO THE COUNTRY

The swallows in their torpid state
Compose their useless wing,
And bees in hives as idly wait
The call of early Spring.

The keenest frost that binds the stream,
The wildest wind that blows,
Are neither felt nor fear'd by them,
Secure of their repose.

But man, all feeling and awake,
The gloomy scene surveys;
With present ills his heart must ache,
And pant for brighter days.

Old Winter, halting o'er the mead,
Bids me and Mary mourn;
But lovely Spring peeps o'er his head,
And whispers your return.

Then April, with her sister May,
Shall chase him from the bowers,
And weave fresh garlands every day,
To crown the smiling hours.

And if a tear that speaks regret
Of happier times, appear,
A glimpse of joy, that we have met,
Shall shine, and dry the tear.

CATHARINA. ADDRESSED TO MISS STAPLETON, (NOW MRS. COURTNEY)

She came—she is gone—we have met—
And meet perhaps never again;
The sun of that moment is set,
And seems to have risen in vain.
Catharina has fled like a dream—
(So vanishes pleasure, alas!)
But has left a regret and esteem
That will not so suddenly pass.

The last evening ramble we made,
Catharina, Maria, and I,
Our progress was often delay'd
By the nightingale warbling nigh.
We paused under many a tree,
And much she was charm'd with a tone,
Less sweet to Maria and me,
Who so lately had witnessed her own.

My numbers that day she had sung,
And gave them a grace so divine,
As only her musical tongue
Could infuse into numbers of mine.
The longer I heard, I esteem'd
The work of my fancy the more,
And e'en to myself never seem'd
So tuneful a poet before.

Though the pleasures of London exceed
In number the days of the year,
Catharina, did nothing impede,
Would feel herself happier here;
For the close-woven arches of limes
On the banks of our river, I know,

Are sweeter to her many times
Than aught that the city can show.

So it is when the mind is endued
With a well-judging taste from above,
Then, whether embellish'd or rude,
'Tis nature alone that we love.
The achievements of art may amuse,
May even our wonder excite;
But groves, hills, and valleys diffuse
A lasting, a sacred delight.

Since then in the rural recess
Catharina alone can rejoice,
May it still be her lot to possess
The scene of her sensible choice!
To inhabit a mansion remote
From the clatter of street-pacing steeds,
And by Philomel's annual note
To measure the life that she leads.

With her book, and her voice, and her lyre,
To wing all her moments at home;
And with scenes that new rapture inspire,
As oft as it suits her to roam;
She will have just the life she prefers,
With little to hope or to fear,
And ours would be pleasant as hers,
Might we view her enjoying it here.

THE MORALIZER CORRECTED. A TALE

A hermit, (or if 'chance you hold
That title now too trite and old,)
A man, once young, who lived retired
As hermit could have well desired,
His hours of study closed at last,
And finish'd his concise repast,
Stoppled his cruise, replaced his book,
Within its customary nook,
And, staff in hand, set forth to share
The sober cordial of sweet air,
Like Isaac, with a mind applied
To serious thought at evening-tide.
Autumnal rains had made it chill,
And from the trees, that fringed his hill,

Shades slanting at the close of day,
Chill'd more his else delightful way.
Distant a little mile he spied
A western bank's still sunny side,
And right toward the favour'd place
Proceeding with his nimblest pace,
In hope to bask a little yet,
Just reach'd it when the sun was set.
    Your hermit, young and jovial sirs!
Learns something from whate'er occurs—
And hence, he said, my mind computes
The real worth of man's pursuits.
His object chosen, wealth or fame,
Or other sublunary game,
Imagination to his view
Presents it deck'd with every hue,
That can seduce him not to spare
His powers of best exertion there,
But youth, health, vigour to expend
On so desirable an end.
Ere long approach life's evening shades
The glow that fancy gave it fades;
And, earn'd too late, it wants the grace
That first engaged him in the chase.
    True, answer'd an angelic guide,
Attendant at the senior's side—
But whether all the time it cost,
To urge the fruitless chase be lost,
Must be decided by the worth
Of that which call'd his ardour forth.
Trifles pursued, whate'er the event,
Must cause him shame or discontent;
A vicious object still is worse,
Successful there, he wins a curse;
But he, whom e'en in life's last stage
Endeavours laudable engage,
Is paid at least in peace of mind,
And sense of having well design'd;
And if, ere he attain his end,
His sun precipitate descend,
A brighter prize than that he meant
Shall recompense his mere intent.
No virtuous wish can bear a date
Either too early or too late.

THE FAITHFUL BIRD

The greenhouse is my summer seat;
My shrubs displaced from that retreat
Enjoy'd the open air;
Two goldfinches, whose sprightly song
Had been their mutual solace long,
Lived happy prisoners there.

They sang as blithe as finches sing,
That flutter loose on golden wing,
And frolic where they list;
Strangers to liberty, 'tis true,
But that delight they never knew,
And therefore never miss'd.

But nature works in every breast,
With force not easily suppress'd;
And Dick felt some desires,
That, after many an effort vain,
Instructed him at length to gain
A pass between his wires.

The open windows seem'd to invite
The freeman to a farewell flight;
But Tom was still confined;
And Dick, although his way was clear,
Was much too generous and sincere
To leave his friend behind.

So settling on his cage, by play,
And chirp, and kiss, he seem'd to say,
You must not live alone—
Nor would he quit that chosen stand
Till I, with slow and cautious hand,
Return'd him to his own.

O ye, who never taste the joys
Of Friendship, satisfied with noise,
Fandango, ball, and rout!
Blush when I tell you how a bird
A prison with a friend preferr'd
To liberty without.

THE NEEDLESS ALARM. A TALE

There is a field, through which I often pass,

Thick overspread with moss and silky grass,
Adjoining close to Kilwick's echoing wood,
Where oft the bitch-fox hides her hapless brood,
Reserved to solace many a neighbouring squire,
That he may follow them through brake and brier,
Contusion hazarding of neck, or spine,
Which rural gentlemen call sport divine.
A narrow brook, by rushy banks conceal'd,
Runs in a bottom, and divides the field;
Oaks intersperse it, that had once a head,
But now wear crests of oven-wood instead;
And where the land slopes to its watery bourn
Wide yawns a gulf beside a ragged thorn;
Bricks line the sides, but shiver'd long ago,
And horrid brambles intertwine below;
A hollow scoop'd, I judge, in ancient time,
For baking earth, or burning rock to lime.

  Not yet the hawthorn bore her berries red,
With which the fieldfare, wintry guest, is fed;
Nor Autumn yet had brush'd from every spray,
With her chill hand, the mellow leaves away;
But corn was housed, and beans were in the stack,
Now therefore issued forth the spotted pack,
With tails high mounted, ears hung low, and throats
With a whole gamut fill'd of heavenly notes,
For which, alas! my destiny severe,
Though ears she gave me two, gave me no ear.

  The sun, accomplishing his early march,
His lamp now planted on heaven's topmost arch,
When, exercise and air my only aim,
And heedless whither, to that field I came,
Ere yet with ruthless joy the happy hound
Told hill and dale that Reynard's track was found,
Or with the high-raised horn's melodious clang
All Kilwick and all Dinglederry rang.

Sheep grazed the field; some with soft bosom press'd
The herb as soft, while nibbling stray'd the rest;
Nor noise was heard but of the hasty brook,
Struggling, detain'd in many a petty nook.
All seem'd so peaceful, that, from them convey'd,
To me their peace by kind contagion spread.

  But when the huntsman, with distended cheek,
'Gan make his instrument of music speak,
And from within the wood that crash was heard,
Though not a hound from whom it burst appear'd,
The sheep recumbent and the sheep that grazed,
All huddling into phalanx, stood and gazed,

Admiring, terrified, the novel strain,
Then coursed the field around, and coursed it round again;
But recollecting, with a sudden thought,
That flight in circles urged advanced them nought,
They gathered close around the old pit's brink,
And thought again—but knew not what to think.
  The man to solitude accustom'd long,
Perceives in every thing that lives a tongue;
Not animals alone, but shrubs and trees
Have speech for him, and understood with ease;
After long drought, when rains abundant fall,
He hears the herbs and flowers rejoicing all;
Knows what the freshness of their hue implies,
How glad they catch the largess of the skies;
But, with precision nicer still, the mind
He scans of every locomotive kind;
Birds of all feather, beasts of every name;
That serve mankind, or shun them, wild or tame;
The looks and gestures of their griefs and fears
Have all articulation in his ears;
He spells them true by intuition's light,
And needs no glossary to set him right.
  This truth premised was needful as a text,
To win due credence to what follows next.
Awhile they mused; surveying every face,
Thou hadst supposed them of superior race;
Their periwigs of wool and fears combined,
Stamp'd on each countenance such marks of mind,
That sage they seem'd, as lawyers o'er a doubt,
Which, puzzling long, at last they puzzle out;
Or academic tutors, teaching youths,
Sure ne'er to want them, mathematic truths;
When thus a mutton statelier than the rest,
A ram, the ewes and wethers sad address'd.
  Friends! we have lived too long. I never heard
Sounds such as these, so worthy to be fear'd.
Could I believe, that winds for ages pent
In earth's dark womb have found at last a vent,
And from their prison-house below arise,
With all these hideous howlings to the skies,
I could be much composed, nor should appear,
For such a cause to feel the slightest fear.
Yourselves have seen, what time the thunders roll'd
All night, me resting quiet in the fold.
Or heard we that tremendous bray alone,
I could expound the melancholy tone;
Should deem it by our old companion made,
The ass; for he, we know, has lately stray'd,

And, being lost, perhaps, and wandering wide,
Might be supposed to clamour for a guide.
But ah! those dreadful yells what soul can hear,
That owns a carcass, and not quake for fear?
Demons produce them doubtless, brazen-claw'd
And fang'd with brass the demons are abroad;
I hold it therefore wisest and most fit
That, life to save, we leap into the pit.

   Him answer'd then his loving mate and true,
But more discreet than he, a Cambrian ewe.

   How! leap into the pit our life to save?
To save our life leap all into the grave?
For can we find it less? Contemplate first
The depth how awful! falling there, we burst:
Or should the brambles, interposed, our fall
In part abate, that happiness were small;
For with a race like theirs no chance I see
Of peace or ease to creatures clad as we.
Meantime, noise kills not. Be it Dapple's bray,
Or be it not, or be it whose it may,
And rush those other sounds, that seem by tongues
Of demons utter'd, from whatever lungs,
Sounds are but sounds, and, till the cause appear,
We have at least commodious standing here.
Come fiend, come fury, giant, monster, blast
From earth or hell, we can but plunge at last.

   While thus she spake, I fainter heard the peals,
For Reynard, close attended at his heels
By panting dog, tired man, and spatter'd horse,
Through mere good fortune, took a different course.
The flock grew calm again, and I, the road
Following, that led me to my own abode,
Much wonder'd that the silly sheep had found
Such cause of terror in an empty sound,
So sweet to huntsman, gentleman, and hound.

MORAL

Beware of desperate steps. The darkest day,
Live till to-morrow, will have pass'd away.

BOADICEA. AN ODE

When the British warrior queen,
Bleeding from the Roman rods,
Sought with an indignant mien,

Counsel of her country's gods,

Sage beneath the spreading oak
Sat the Druid, hoary chief;
Every burning word he spoke
Full of rage, and full of grief.

Princess! if our aged eyes
Weep upon thy matchless wrongs,
'Tis because resentment ties
All the terrors of our tongues.

Rome shall perish—write that word
In the blood that she has spilt;
Perish, hopeless and abhorr'd,
Deep in ruin as in guilt.

Rome, for empire far renown'd,
Tramples on a thousand states;
Soon her pride shall kiss the ground
Hark! the Gaul is at her gates!

Other Romans shall arise,
Heedless of a soldier's name;
Sounds, not arms, shall win the prize,
Harmony the path to fame.

Then the progeny that springs
From the forests of our land,
Arm'd with thunder, clad with wings,
Shall a wider world command.

Regions Cæsar never knew
Thy posterity shall sway;
Where his eagles never flew,
None invincible as they.

Such the bard's prophetic words,
Pregnant with celestial fire,
Bending as he swept the chords
Of his sweet but awful lyre.

She, with all a monarch's pride,
Felt them in her bosom glow:
Rush'd to battle, fought, and died;
Dying, hurl'd them at the foe.

Ruffians, pitiless as proud,

Heaven awards the vengeance due;
Empire is on us bestow'd,
Shame and ruin wait for you.

HEROISM

There was a time when Ætna's silent fire
Slept unperceiv'd, the mountain yet entire;
When, conscious of no danger from below,
She tower'd a cloud-capt pyramid of snow.
No thunders shook with deep intestine sound
The blooming groves that girdled her around.
Her unctuous olives, and her purple vines
(Unfelt the fury of those bursting mines)
The peasant's hopes, and not in vain, assured,
In peace upon her sloping sides matured.
When on a day, like that of the last doom,
A conflagration labouring in her womb,
She teem'd and heaved with an infernal birth,
That shook the circling seas and solid earth.
Dark and voluminous the vapours rise,
And hang their horrors in the neighbouring skies,
While through the Stygian veil, that blots the day,
In dazzling streaks the vivid lightnings play.
But oh! what muse, and in what powers of song,
Can trace the torrent as it burns along?
Havoc and devastation in the van,
It marches o'er the prostrate works of man;
Vines, olives, herbage, forests disappear,
And all the charms of a Sicilian year.
  Revolving seasons, fruitless as they pass,
See it an uninformed and idle mass;
Without a soil to invite the tiller's care,
Or blade that might redeem it from despair.
Yet time at length (what will not time achieve?)
Clothes it with earth, and bids the produce live.
Once more the spiry myrtle crowns the glade,
And ruminating flocks enjoy the shade.
O bliss precarious, and unsafe retreats,
O charming Paradise of shortlived sweets!
The self-same gale that wafts the fragrance round
Brings to the distant ear a sullen sound:
Again the mountain feels the imprison'd foe,
Again pours ruin on the vale below.
Ten thousand swains the wasted scene deplore,
That only future ages can restore.

Ye monarchs, whom the lure of honour draws,
Who write in blood the merits of your cause,
Who strike the blow, then plead your own defence,
Glory your aim, but justice your pretence;
Behold in Ætna's emblematic fires
The mischiefs your ambitious pride inspires!
    Fast by the stream that bounds your just domain,
And tells you where you have a right to reign,
A nation dwells, not envious of your throne,
Studious of peace, their neighbour's and their own,
Ill-fated race! how deeply must they rue
Their only crime, vicinity to you!
The trumpet sounds, your legions swarm abroad,
Through the ripe harvest lies their destined road;
At every step beneath their feet they tread
The life of multitudes, a nation's bread!
Earth seems a garden in its loveliest dress
Before them, and behind a wilderness.
Famine, and Pestilence, her firstborn son,
Attend to finish what the sword begun;
And echoing praises, such as fiends might earn,
And folly pays, resound at your return.
A calm succeeds—but Plenty, with her train
Of heartfelt joys, succeeds not soon again:
And years of pining indigence must show
What scourges are the gods that rule below.
    Yet man, laborious man, by slow degrees,
(Such is his thirst of opulence and ease,)
Plies all the sinews of industrious toil,
Gleans up the refuse of the general spoil,
Rebuilds the towers that smoked upon the plain,
And the sun gilds the shining spires again.
    Increasing commerce and reviving art
Renew the quarrel on the conqueror's part;
And the sad lesson must be learn'd once more,
That wealth within is ruin at the door.
What are ye, monarchs, laurell'd heroes, say,
But Ætnas of the suffering world ye sway?
Sweet Nature, stripp'd of her embroider'd robe,
Deplores the wasted regions of her globe;
And stands a witness at Truth's awful bar,
To prove you there destroyers as ye are.
    O place me in some heaven-protected isle,
Where Peace, and Equity, and Freedom smile;
Where no volcano pours his fiery flood,
No crested warrior dips his plume in blood;
Where Power secures what Industry has won;
Where to succeed is not to be undone;

A land that distant tyrants hate in vain,
In Britain's isle, beneath a George's reign.

ON THE RECEIPT OF MY MOTHER'S PICTURE OUT OF NORFOLK, THE GIFT OF MY COUSIN, ANN BODHAM

O that those lips had language! Life has pass'd
With me but roughly since I heard thee last.
Those lips are thine—thy own sweet smile I see,
The same that oft in childhood solaced me;
Voice only fails, else how distinct they say,
"Grieve not, my child, chase all thy fears away!"
The meek intelligence of those dear eyes
(Blest be the art that can immortalize,
The art that baffles Time's tyrannic claim
To quench it) here shines on me still the same.
   Faithful remembrancer of one so dear,
O welcome guest, though unexpected here:
Who bidst me honour with an artless song,
Affectionate, a mother lost so long.
I will obey, not willingly alone,
But gladly, as the precept were her own:
And, while that face renews my filial grief,
Fancy shall weave a charm for my relief,
Shall steep me in Elysian reverie,
A momentary dream, that thou art she.
   My mother! when I learn'd that thou wast dead,
Say, wast thou conscious of the tears I shed?
Hover'd thy spirit o'er thy sorrowing son,
Wretch even then, life's journey just begun?
Perhaps thou gavest me, though unfelt, a kiss;
Perhaps a tear, if souls can weep in bliss—
Ah, that maternal smile! it answers—Yes.
I heard the bell toll'd on thy burial day,
I saw the hearse that bore thee slow away,
And turning from my nursery window, drew
A long, long sigh, and wept a last adieu!
But was it such?—It was.—Where thou art gone
Adieus and farewells are a sound unknown.
May I but meet thee on that peaceful shore,
The parting word shall pass my lips no more!
Thy maidens, grieved themselves at my concern,
Oft gave me promise of thy quick return.
What ardently I wish'd, I long believed,
And, disappointed still, was still deceived.
By expectation every day beguiled,

Dupe of to-morrow even from a child.
Thus many a sad to-morrow came and went,
Till, all my stock of infant sorrows spent,
I learn'd at last submission to my lot,
But, though I less deplored thee, ne'er forgot.
   Where once we dwelt our name is heard no more,
Children not thine have trod my nursery floor;
And where the gardener Robin, day by day,
Drew me to school along the public way,
Delighted with my bauble coach, and wrapp'd
In scarlet mantle warm, and velvet capp'd,
'Tis now become a history little known,
That once we call'd the pastoral house our own.
Short-lived possession! but the record fair,
That memory keeps of all thy kindness there,
Still outlives many a storm, that has effaced
A thousand other themes less deeply traced.
Thy nightly visits to my chamber made,
That thou mightst know me safe and warmly laid;
Thy morning bounties ere I left my home,
The biscuit or confectionary plum;
The fragrant waters on my cheeks bestow'd
By thy own hand, till fresh they shone and glow'd:
All this, and more endearing still than all,
Thy constant flow of love that knew no fall,
Ne'er roughen'd by those cataracts and breaks
That humour interposed too often makes;
All this still legible in memory's page,
And still to be so to my latest age,
Adds joy to duty, makes me glad to pay
Such honours to thee as my numbers may;
Perhaps a frail memorial, but sincere,
Not scorn'd in heaven, though little noticed here.
   Could Time, his flight reversed, restore the hours,
When, playing with thy vesture's tissued flowers,
The violet, the pink, and jessamine,
I prick'd them into paper with a pin,
(And thou wast happier than myself the while,
Wouldst softly speak, and stroke my head, and smile,)
Could those few pleasant days again appear,
Might one wish bring them, would I wish them here?
I would not trust my heart—the dear delight
Seems so to be desired, perhaps I might.—
But no—what here we call our life is such,
So little to be loved, and thou so much,
That I should ill requite thee to constrain
Thy unbound spirit into bonds again.
   Thou, as a gallant bark from Albion's coast

(The storms all weather'd and the ocean cross'd)
Shoots into port at some well-haven'd isle
Where spices breathe, and brighter seasons smile,
There sits quiescent on the floods, that show
Her beauteous form reflected clear below,
While airs impregnated with incense play
Around her, fanning light her streamers gay:
So thou, with sails how swift! hast reach'd the shore,
"Where tempests never beat nor billows roar;"
And thy loved consort on the dangerous tide
Of life long since has anchor'd by thy side.
But me, scarce hoping to attain that rest,
Always from port withheld, always distress'd—
Me howling blasts drive devious, tempest-toss'd
Sails ripp'd, seams opening wide, and compass lost,
And day by day some current's thwarting force
Sets me more distant from a prosperous course.
But oh, the thought, that thou art safe, and he!
That thought is joy, arrive what may to me.
My boast is not that I deduce my birth
From loins enthroned, and rulers of the earth;
But higher far my proud pretensions rise—
The son of parents pass'd into the skies.
And now, farewell—Time unrevoked has run
His wonted course, yet what I wish'd is done.
By contemplation's help, not sought in vain,
I seem to have lived my childhood o'er again;
To have renew'd the joys that once were mine,
Without the sin of violating thine;
And, while the wings of fancy still are free,
And I can view this mimic show of thee,
Time has but half succeeded in his theft—
Thyself removed, thy power to soothe me left.

FRIENDSHIP

What virtue, or what mental grace
But men unqualified and base
Will boast it their possession?
Profusion apes the noble part
Of liberality of heart,
And dullness of discretion.

If every polish'd gem we find,
Illuminating heart or mind,
Provoke to imitation;

No wonder friendship does the same,
That jewel of the purest flame,
Or rather constellation.

No knave but boldly will pretend
The requisites that form a friend,
A real and a sound one;
Nor any fool, he would deceive,
But prove as ready to believe,
And dream that he had found one.

Candid, and generous, and just,
Boys care but little whom they trust,
An error soon corrected—
For who but learns in riper years
That man, when smoothest he appears,
Is most to be suspected?

But here again a danger lies,
Lest, having misapplied our eyes,
And taken trash for treasure,
We should unwarily conclude
Friendship a false ideal good,
A mere Utopian pleasure.

An acquisition rather rare
Is yet no subject of despair;
Nor is it wise complaining,
If, either on forbidden ground,
Or where it was not to be found,
We sought without attaining.

No friendship will abide the test,
That stands on sordid interest,
Or mean self-love erected;
Nor such as may awhile subsist
Between the sot and sensualist,
For vicious ends connected.

Who seek a friend should come disposed
To exhibit, in full bloom disclosed,
The graces and the beauties
That form the character he seeks,
For 'tis a union that bespeaks
Reciprocated duties.

Mutual attention is implied,
And equal truth on either side,

And constantly supported;
'Tis senseless arrogance to accuse
Another of sinister views,
Our own as much distorted.

But will sincerity suffice?
It is indeed above all price,
And must be made the basis;
But every virtue of the soul
Must constitute the charming whole,
All shining in their places.

A fretful temper will divide
The closest knot that may be tied,
By ceaseless sharp corrosion;
A temper passionate and fierce
May suddenly your joys disperse
At one immense explosion.

In vain the talkative unite
In hopes of permanent delight—
The secret just committed,
Forgetting its important weight,
They drop through mere desire to prate,
And by themselves outwitted.

How bright soe'er the prospect seems,
All thoughts of friendship are but dreams,
If envy chance to creep in;
An envious man, if you succeed,
May prove a dangerous foe indeed,
But not a friend worth keeping.

As envy pines at good possess'd,
So jealousy looks forth distress'd
On good that seems approaching;
And, if success his steps attend,
Discerns a rival in a friend,
And hates him for encroaching.

Hence authors of illustrious name,
Unless belied by common fame,
Are sadly prone to quarrel,
To deem the wit a friend displays
A tax upon their own just praise,
And pluck each other's laurel.

A man renown'd for repartee

Will seldom scruple to make free
With friendship's finest feeling,
Will thrust a dagger at your breast,
And say he wounded you in jest,
By way of balm for healing.

Whoever keeps an open ear
For tattlers will be sure to hear
The trumpet of contention;
Aspersion is the babbler's trade,
To listen is to lend him aid,
And rush into dissension.

A friendship that in frequent fits
Of controversial rage emits
The sparks of disputation,
Like hand-in-hand insurance-plates,
Most unavoidably creates
The thought of conflagration.

Some fickle creatures boast a soul
True as a needle to the pole,
Their humour yet so various—
They manifest their whole life through
The needle's deviations too,
Their love is so precarious.

The great and small but rarely meet
On terms of amity complete;
Plebeians must surrender,
And yield so much to noble folk,
It is combining fire with smoke,
Obscurity with splendour.

Some are so placid and serene
(As Irish bogs are always green)
They sleep secure from waking;
And are indeed a bog, that bears
Your unparticipated cares
Unmoved and without quaking.

Courtier and patriot cannot mix
Their heterogeneous politics
Without an effervescence,
Like that of salts with lemon juice,
Which does not yet like that produce
A friendly coalescence.

Religion should extinguish strife,
And make a calm of human life;
But friends that chance to differ
On points which God has left at large,
How freely will they meet and charge
No combatants are stiffer.

To prove at last my main intent
Needs no expense of argument,
No cutting and contriving—
Seeking a real friend, we seem
To adopt the chemist's golden dream,
With still less hope of thriving.

Sometimes the fault is all our own,
Some blemish in due time made known
By trespass or omission;
Sometimes occasion brings to light
Our friend's defect, long hid from sight,
And even from suspicion.

Then judge yourself, and prove your man
As circumspectly as you can,
And, having made election,
Beware no negligence of yours,
Such as a friend but ill endures,
Enfeeble his affection.

That secrets are a sacred trust,
That friends should be sincere and just,
That constancy befits them,
Are observations on the case,
That savour much of common place,
And all the world admits them.

But 'tis not timber, lead, and stone,
An architect requires alone
To finish a fine building—
The palace were but half complete,
If he could possibly forget
The carving and the gilding.

The man that hails you Tom or Jack,
And proves by thumps upon your back
How he esteems your merit,
Is such a friend, that one had need
Be very much his friend indeed
To pardon or to bear it.

As similarity of mind,
Or something not to be defined,
First fixes our attention;
So manners decent and polite,
The same we practised at first sight,
Must save it from declension.

Some act upon this prudent plan,
"Say little, and hear all you can."
Safe policy, but hateful—
So barren sands imbibe the shower,
But render neither fruit nor flower,
Unpleasant and ungrateful.

The man I trust, if shy to me,
Shall find me as reserved as he,
No subterfuge or pleading
Shall win my confidence again;
I will by no means entertain
A spy on my proceeding.

These samples—for alas! at last
These are but samples, and a taste
Of evils yet unmention'd—
May prove the task a task indeed,
In which 'tis much if we succeed,
However well intention'd.

Pursue the search, and you will find
Good sense and knowledge of mankind
To be at least expedient,
And, after summing all the rest,
Religion ruling in the breast
A principal ingredient.

The noblest Friendship ever shown
The Saviour's history makes known,
Though some have turn'd and turn'd it;
And, whether being crazed or blind,
Or seeking with a biass'd mind,
Have not, it seems, discern'd it.

O Friendship! if my soul forego
Thy dear delights while here below,
To mortify and grieve me,
May I myself at last appear
Unworthy, base, and insincere,

Or may my friend deceive me!

ON A MISCHIEVOUS BULL, WHICH THE OWNER OF HIM SOLD AT THE AUTHOR'S INSTANCE

Go—thou art all unfit to share
The pleasures of this place
With such as its old tenants are,
Creatures of gentler race.

The squirrel here his hoard provides,
Aware of wintry storms,
And woodpeckers explore the sides
Of rugged oaks for worms.

The sheep here smooths the knotted thorn
With frictions of her fleece;
And here I wander eve and morn,
Like her, a friend to peace.

Ah!—I could pity thee exiled
From this secure retreat—
I would not lose it to be styled
The happiest of the great.

But thou canst taste no calm delight;
Thy pleasure is to show
Thy magnanimity in fight,
Thy prowess—therefore, go—

I care not whether east or north,
So I no more may find thee;
The angry muse thus sings thee forth,
And claps the gate behind thee.

ANNUS MEMORABILIS, 1789. WRITTEN IN COMMEMORATION OF HIS MAJESTY'S HAPPY RECOVERY

I ransack'd for a theme of song,
Much ancient chronicle, and long;
I read of bright embattled fields,
Of trophied helmets, spears, and shields,
Of chiefs, whose single arm could boast
Prowess to dissipate a host;
Through tomes of fable and of dream
I sought an eligible theme,

But none I found, or found them shared
Already by some happier bard.
   To modern times, with truth to guide
My busy search, I next applied;
Here cities won, and fleets dispersed,
Urged loud a claim to be rehearsed,
Deeds of unperishing renown,
Our fathers' triumphs and our own.
   Thus as the bee, from bank to bower,
Assiduous sips at every flower,
But rests on none till that be found
Where most nectareous sweets abound,
So I, from theme to theme display'd
In many a page historic, stray'd,
Siege after siege, fight after fight,
Contemplating with small delight,
(For feats of sanguinary hue
Not always glitter in my view,)
Till, settling on the current year,
I found the far-sought treasure near.
A theme for poetry divine,
A theme to ennoble even mine,
In memorable eighty-nine.
   The spring of eighty-nine shall be
An æra cherish'd long by me,
Which joyful I will oft record,
And thankful at my frugal board;
For then the clouds of eighty-eight,
That threaten'd England's trembling state
With loss of what she least could spare,
Her sovereign's tutelary care,
One breath of heaven, that cried—Restore!
Chased, never to assemble more:
And for the richest crown on earth,
If valued by its wearer's worth,
The symbol of a righteous reign
Sat fast on George's brows again.
   Then peace and joy again possess'd
Our Queen's long-agitated breast;
Such joy and peace as can be known
By sufferers like herself alone,
Who losing, or supposing lost,
The good on earth they valued most,
For that dear sorrow's sake forego
All hope of happiness below,
Then suddenly regain the prize,
And flash thanksgivings to the skies!
   O Queen of Albion, queen of isles!

Since all thy tears were changed to smiles,
The eyes, that never saw thee, shine
With joy not unallied to thine;
Transports not chargeable with art
Illume the land's remotest part,
And strangers to the air of courts,
Both in their toils and at their sports,
The happiness of answer'd prayers,
That gilds thy features, show in theirs.
    If they who on thy state attend,
Awe-struck, before thy presence bend,
'Tis but the natural effect
Of grandeur that ensures respect;
But she is something more than queen
Who is beloved where never seen.

HYMN, FOR THE USE OF THE SUNDAY SCHOOL AT OLNEY

Hear, Lord, the song of praise and prayer,
In heaven thy dwelling place,
From infants made the public care,
And taught to seek thy face.

Thanks for thy word, and for thy day,
And grant us, we implore,
Never to waste in sinful play
Thy holy sabbaths more.

Thanks that we hear,—but O impart
To each desires sincere,
That we may listen with our heart,
And learn as well as hear.

For if vain thoughts the minds engage
Of older far than we,
What hope, that, at our heedless age,
Our minds should e'er be free?

Much hope, if thou our spirits take
Under thy gracious sway,
Who canst the wisest wiser make,
And babes as wise as they.

Wisdom and bliss thy word bestows,
A sun that ne'er declines,
And be thy mercies shower'd on those

Who placed us where it shines.

STANZAS

SUBJOINED TO THE YEARLY BILL OF MORTALITY OF THE PARISH OF ALL-SAINTS, NORTHAMPTON, ANNO DOMINI 1787

Pallida mors æquo pulsat pede pauperum tabernas,
Regumque turres. —Horace.

Pale death with equal foot strikes wide the door
Of royal halls and hovels of the poor.

While thirteen moons saw smoothly run
The Nen's barge-laden wave,
All these, life's rambling journey done,
Have found their home, the grave.

Was man (frail always) made more frail
Than in foregoing years?
Did famine or did plague prevail,
That so much death appears?

No; these were vigorous as their sires,
Nor plague nor famine came;
This annual tribute Death requires,
And never waves his claim.

Like crowded forest trees we stand,
And some are mark'd to fall;
The axe will smite at God's command,
And soon shall smite us all.

Green as the bay tree, ever green,
With its new foliage on,
The gay, the thoughtless, have I seen,
I pass'd—and they were gone.

Read, ye that run, the awful truth
With which I charge my page;
A worm is in the bud of youth,
And at the root of age.

No present health can health ensure
For yet an hour to come;
No medicine, though it oft can cure,

Can always balk the tomb.

And O! that humble as my lot,
And scorn'd as is my strain,
These truths, though known, too much forgot,
I may not teach in vain.

So prays your clerk with all his heart,
And, ere he quits the pen,
Begs you for once to take his part,
And answer all—Amen!

ON A SIMILAR OCCASION. FOR THE YEAR 1788.

Quod adest, memento
Componere æquus. Cætera fluminis
Ritu feruntur.—
Horace.

Improve the present hour, for all beside
Is a mere feather on a torrent's tide.
. . . .

Could I, from heaven inspired, as sure presage
To whom the rising year shall prove his last,
As I can number in my punctual page,
And item down the victims of the past;

How each would trembling wait the mournful sheet,
On which the press might stamp him next to die;
And, reading here his sentence, how replete
With anxious meaning, heavenward turn his eye!

Time then would seem more precious than the joys
In which he sports away the treasure now;
And prayer more seasonable than the noise
Of drunkards, or the music-drawing bow.

Then doubtless many a trifler, on the brink
Of this world's hazardous and headlong shore,
Forced to a pause, would feel it good to think,
Told that his setting sun must rise no more.

Ah self-deceived! Could I prophetic say
Who next is fated, and who next to fall,
The rest might then seem privileged to play;

But, naming none, the Voice now speaks to All.

Observe the dappled foresters, how light
They bound and airy o'er the sunny glade—
One falls—the rest, wide scatter'd with affright,
Vanish at once into the darkest shade.

Had we their wisdom, should we, often warn'd,
Still need repeated warnings, and at last,
A thousand awful admonitions scorn'd,
Die self-accused of life run all to waste!

Sad waste! for which no after-thrift atones.
The grave admits no cure for guilt or sin;
Dewdrops may deck the turf that hides the bones,
But tears of godly grief ne'er flow within.

Learn then, ye living! by the mouths be taught
Of all these sepulchres, instructors true,
That, soon or late, death also is your lot,
And the next opening grave may yawn for you.

ON A SIMILAR OCCASION. FOR THE YEAR 1789

—*Placidâque ibi demum morte quievit.*—*Virg.*

There calm at length he breathed his soul away.

"O most delightful hour by man
Experienced here below,
The hour that terminates his span,
His folly and his woe!

"Worlds should not bribe me back to tread
Again life's dreary waste,
To see again my day o'erspread
With all the gloomy past.

"My home henceforth is in the skies,
Earth, seas, and sun, adieu!
All heaven unfolded to my eyes,
I have no sight for you."

So spake Aspasio, firm possess'd
Of faith's supporting rod,
Then breathed his soul into its rest,

The bosom of his God.

He was a man among the few
Sincere on virtue's side;
And all his strength from Scripture drew,
To hourly use applied.

That rule he prized, by that he fear'd,
He hated, hoped, and loved;
Nor ever frown'd, or sad appear'd,
But when his heart had roved.

For he was frail as thou or I,
And evil felt within;
But when he felt it, heaved a sigh,
And loathed the thought of sin.

Such lived Aspasio; and at last
Call'd up from earth to heaven,
The gulf of death triumphant pass'd,
By gales of blessing driven.

His joys be mine, each reader cries,
When my last hour arrives:
They shall be yours, my verse replies,
Such only be your lives.

ON A SIMILAR OCCASION. FOR THE YEAR 1790

Ne commonentem recta sperne. —*Buchanan.*

Despise not my good counsel.

He who sits from day to day
Where the prison'd lark is hung,
Heedless of his loudest lay,
Hardly knows that he has sung.

Where the watchman in his round
Nightly lifts his voice on high,
None, accustom'd to the sound,
Wakes the sooner for his cry.

So your verse-man I, and clerk,
Yearly in my song proclaim
Death at hand—yourselves his mark—

And the foe's unerring aim.

Duly at my time I come,
Publishing to all aloud—
Soon the grave must be your home,
And your only suit, a shroud,

But the monitory strain,
Oft repeated in your ears,
Seems to sound too much in vain,
Wins no notice, wakes no fears.

Can a truth, by all confess'd
Of such magnitude and weight,
Grow, by being oft impress'd,
Trivial as a parrot's prate?

Pleasure's call attention wins,
Hear it often as we may;
New as ever seem our sins,
Though committed every day.

Death and judgment, heaven and hell—
These alone, so often heard,
No more move us than the bell
When some stranger is interr'd.

O then, ere the turf or tomb
Cover us from every eye,
Spirit of instruction, come,
Make us learn that we must die.

ON A SIMILAR OCCASION, FOR THE YEAR 1792

Felix, qui potuit rerum cognoscere causas,
Atque metus omnes et inexorabile fatum
Subjecit pedibus, strepitumque Acherontis avari!
Virg.

Happy the mortal who has traced effects
To their first cause, cast fear beneath his feet,
And death and roaring hell's voracious fires!

Thankless for favours from on high,
Man thinks he fades too soon;
Though 'tis his privilege to die,

Would he improve the boon.

But he, not wise enough to scan
His blest concerns aright,
Would gladly stretch life's little span
To ages, if he might.

To ages in a world of pain,
To ages, where he goes
Gall'd by affliction's heavy chain,
And hopeless of repose.

Strange fondness of the human heart,
Enamour'd of its harm!
Strange world, that costs it so much smart,
And still has power to charm.

Whence has the world her magic power?
Why deem we death a foe?
Recoil from weary life's best hour,
And covet longer woe?

The cause is Conscience—Conscience oft
Her tale of guilt renews:
Her voice is terrible though soft,
And dread of death ensues.

Then anxious to be longer spared
Man mourns his fleeting breath:
All evils then seem light, compared
With the approach of death.

'Tis judgment shakes him: there's the fear
That prompts the wish to stay:
He has incurr'd a long arrear,
And must despair to pay.

Pay!—follow Christ, and all is paid;
is death your peace ensures;
Think on the grave where he was laid,
And calm descend to yours.

ON A SIMILAR OCCASION. FOR THE YEAR 1793

De sacris autem hæc sit una sententia, ut conserventur.
Cic. de Leg.

But let us all concur in this one sentiment, that things sacred be inviolate.

He lives who lives to God alone,
And all are dead beside;
For other source than God is none
Whence life can be supplied

To live to God is to requite
His love as best we may:
To make his precepts our delight,
His promises our stay.

But life, within a narrow ring
Of giddy joys comprised,
Is falsely named, and no such thing,
But rather death disguised.

Can life in them deserve the name,
Who only live to prove
For what poor toys they can disclaim
An endless life above?

Who, much diseased, yet nothing feel;
Much menaced, nothing dread;
Have wounds, which only God can heal,
Yet never ask his aid?

Who deem his house a useless place,
Faith, want of common sense;
And ardour in the Christian race,
A hypocrite's pretence?

Who trample order; and the day
Which God asserts his own
Dishonour with unhallow'd play,
And worship chance alone?

If scorn of God's commands, impress'd
On word and deed, imply
The better part of man unbless'd
With life that cannot die;

Such want it, and that want uncured
Till man resigns his breath,
Speaks him a criminal, assured
Of everlasting death.

Sad period to a pleasant course!
Yet so will God repay
Sabbaths profaned without remorse,
And mercy cast away.

ON A GOLDFINCH, STARVED TO DEATH IN HIS CAGE

Time was when I was free as air,
The thistle's downy seed my fare,
My drink the morning dew;
I perch'd at will on every spray,
My form genteel, my plumage gay,
My strains for ever new.

But gaudy plumage, sprightly strain,
And form genteel were all in vain,
And of a transient date;
For, caught and caged, and starved to death,
In dying sighs my little breath
Soon pass'd the wiry grate.

Thanks, gentle swain, for all my woes,
And thanks for this effectual close
And cure of every ill!
More cruelty could none express;
And I, if you had shown me less,
Had been your prisoner still.

THE PINE-APPLE AND THE BEE

The pine-apples, in triple row,
Were basking hot, and all in blow;
A bee of most discerning taste
Perceived the fragrance as he pass'd,
On eager wing the spoiler came,
And search'd for crannies in the frame,
Urged his attempt on every side,
To every pane his trunk applied;
But still in vain, the frame was tight,
And only pervious to the light:
Thus having wasted half the day,
He trimm'd his flight another way.
   Methinks, I said, in thee I find
The sin and madness of mankind.

To joys forbidden man aspires,
Consumes his soul with vain desires;
Folly the spring of his pursuit,
And disappointment all the fruit.
While Cynthio ogles, as she passes,
The nymph between two chariot glasses,
She is the pineapple, and he
The silly unsuccessful bee.
The maid who views with pensive air
The show-glass fraught with glittering ware,
Sees watches, bracelets, rings, and lockets,
But sighs at thought of empty pockets;
Like thine, her appetite is keen,
But ah, the cruel glass between!
  Our dear delights are often such,
Exposed to view, but not to touch;
The sight our foolish heart inflames,
We long for pine-apples in frames;
With hopeless wish one looks and lingers;
One breaks the glass, and cuts his fingers;
But they whom truth and wisdom lead
Can gather honey from a weed.

VERSES WRITTEN AT BATH, ON FINDING THE HEEL OF A SHOE

Fortune! I thank thee: gentle goddess! thanks!
Not that my muse, though bashful, shall deny
She would have thank'd thee rather hadst thou cast
A treasure in her way; for neither meed
Of early breakfast, to dispel the fumes,
And bowel-racking pains of emptiness,
Nor noontide feast, nor evening's cool repast,
Hopes she from this—presumptuous, though, perhaps
The cobbler, leather-carving artist! might.
Nathless she thanks thee and accepts thy boon,
Whatever; not as erst the fabled cock,
Vain-glorious fool! unknowing what he found,
Spurn'd the rich gem thou gavest him. Wherefore, ah!
Why not on me that favour, (worthier sure!)
Conferr'dst thou, goddess! Thou art blind thou say'st:
Enough!—thy blindness shall excuse the deed.
  Nor does my muse no benefit exhale
From this thy scant indulgence!—even here
Hints worthy sage philosophy are found;
Illustrious hints, to moralize my song!
This ponderous heel of perforated hide

Compact, with pegs indented, many a row,
Haply (for such its massy form bespeaks)
The weighty tread of some rude peasant clown
Upbore: on this, supported oft, he stretch'd,
With uncouth strides, along the furrow'd glebe,
Flattening the stubborn clod, till cruel time
(What will not cruel time?) on a wry step
Sever'd the strict cohesion; when, alas!
He, who could erst, with even, equal pace,
Pursue his destined way with symmetry,
And some proportion form'd, now on one side
Curtail'd and maim'd, the sport of vagrant boys,
Cursing his frail supporter, treacherous prop!
With toilsome steps, and difficult, moves on.
Thus fares it oft with other than the feet
Of humble villager—the statesman thus,
Up the steep road where proud ambition leads,
Aspiring, first uninterrupted winds
His prosperous way; nor fears miscarriage foul,
While policy prevails, and friends prove true;
But, that support soon failing, by him left
On whom he most depended, basely left,
Betray'd, deserted; from his airy height
Headlong he falls; and through the rest of life
Drags the dull load of disappointment on.

1748.

AN ODE, ON READING RICHARDSON'S HISTORY OF SIR CHARLES GRANDISON

Say, ye apostate and profane,
Wretches, who blush not to disdain
Allegiance to your God,—
Did e'er your idly wasted love
Of virtue for her sake remove
And lift you from the crowd?

Would you the race of glory run,
Know, the devout, and they alone,
Are equal to the task:
The labours of the illustrious course
Far other than the unaided force
Of human vigour ask.

To arm against reputed ill
The patient heart too brave to feel

The tortures of despair:
Nor safer yet high-crested pride,
When wealth flows in with every tide
To gain admittance there.

To rescue from the tyrant's sword
The oppress'd; unseen and unimplored,
To cheer the face of woe;
From lawless insult to defend
An orphan's right—a fallen friend,
And a forgiven foe;

These, these distinguish from the crowd,
And these alone, the great and good,
The guardians of mankind;
Whose bosoms with these virtues heave,
O with what matchless speed they leave
The multitude behind!

Then ask ye, from what cause on earth
Virtues like these derive their birth?
Derived from Heaven alone,
Full on that favour'd breast they shine,
Where faith and resignation join
To call the blessing down.

Such is that heart:—but while the muse
Thy theme, O Richardson, pursues,
Her feeble spirits faint:
She cannot reach, and would not wrong,
The subject for an angel's song,
The hero, and the saint!

1753.

AN EPISTLE TO ROBERT LLOYD, ESQ.

'Tis not that I design to rob
Thee of thy birthright, gentle Bob,
For thou art born sole heir, and single,
Of dear Mat Prior's easy jingle;
Not that I mean, while thus I knit
My threadbare sentiments together,
To show my genius or my wit,
When God and you know I have neither;
Or such as might be better shown

By letting poetry alone.
'Tis not with either of these views
That I presumed to address the muse:
But to divert a fierce banditti,
(Sworn foes to every thing that's witty!)
That, with a black, infernal train,
Make cruel inroads in my brain,
And daily threaten to drive thence
My little garrison of sense;
The fierce banditti which I mean
Are gloomy thoughts led on by spleen.
Then there's another reason yet,
Which is, that I may fairly quit
The debt, which justly became due
The moment when I heard from you;
And you might grumble, crony mine,
If paid in any other coin;
Since twenty sheets of lead, God knows,
(I would say twenty sheets of prose,)
Can ne'er be deem'd worth half so much
As one of gold, and yours was such.
Thus, the preliminaries settled,
I fairly find myself pitchkettled,
And cannot see, though few see better,
How I shall hammer out a letter.
    First, for a thought—since all agree—
A thought—I have it—let me see—
'Tis gone again—plague on't! I thought
I had it—but I have it not.
Dame Gurton thus, and Hodge her son,
That useful thing, her needle, gone!
Rake well the cinders—sweep the floor,
And sift the dust behind the door;
While eager Hodge beholds the prize
In old grimalkin's glaring eyes;
And Gammer finds it, on her knees,
In every shining straw she sees.
This simile were apt enough;
But I've another, critic-proof!
The virtuoso thus, at noon,
Broiling beneath a July sun,
The gilded butterfly pursues,
O'er hedge and ditch, through gaps and mews;
And, after many a vain essay,
To captivate the tempting prey,
Gives him at length the lucky pat,
And has him safe beneath his hat:
Then lifts it gently from the ground;

But, ah! 'tis lost as soon as found;
Culprit his liberty regains,
Flits out of sight, and mocks his pains.
The sense was dark; 'twas therefore fit
With simile to illustrate it;
But as too much obscures the sight,
As often as too little light,
We have our similes cut short,
For matters of more grave import.
That Matthew's numbers run with ease,
Each man of common sense agrees!
All men of common sense allow
That Robert's lines are easy too:
Where then the preference shall we place,
Or how do justice in this case?
Matthew (says Fame,) with endless pains
Smoothed and refined the meanest strains;
Nor suffer'd one ill chosen rhyme
To escape him at the idlest time;
And thus o'er all a lustre cast,
That, while the language lives shall last.
A'nt please your ladyship (quoth I,)
For 'tis my business to reply;
Sure so much labour, so much toil,
Bespeak at least a stubborn soil:
Theirs be the laurel-wreath decreed,
Who both write well, and write full speed!
Who throw their Helicon about
As freely as a conduit spout!
Friend Robert, thus like chien savant
Lets fall a poem en passant,
Nor needs his genuine ore refine—
'Tis ready polish'd from the mine.

A TALE, FOUNDED ON A FACT, WHICH HAPPENED IN JANUARY, 1779

Where Humber pours his rich commercial stream
There dwelt a wretch, who breathed but to blaspheme;
In subterraneous caves his life he led,
Black as the mine in which he wrought for bread.
When on a day, emerging from the deep,
A sabbath-day, (such sabbaths thousands keep!)
The wages of his weekly toil he bore
To buy a cock—whose blood might win him more;
As if the noblest of the feather'd kind
Were but for battle and for death design'd;

As if the consecrated hours were meant
For sport, to minds on cruelty intent;
It chanced (such chances Providence obey)
He met a fellow labourer on the way,
Whose heart the same desires had once inflamed;
But now the savage temper was reclaim'd,
Persuasion on his lips had taken place;
For all plead well who plead the cause of grace.
His iron heart with scripture he assail'd,
Woo'd him to hear a sermon, and prevail'd.
His faithful bow the mighty preacher drew,
Swift as the lightning-glimpse the arrow flew.
He wept; he trembled; cast his eyes around,
To find a worse than he; but none he found.
He felt his sins, and wonder'd he should feel.
Grace made the wound, and grace alone could heal.
　Now farewell oaths, and blasphemies, and lies!
He quits the sinner's for the martyr's prize.
That holy day was wash'd with many a tear,
Gilded with hope, yet shaded too by fear.
The next, his swarthy brethren of the mine
Learn'd, by his altered speech, the change divine!
Laugh'd when they should have wept, and swore the day
Was nigh when he would swear as fast as they.
"No," said the penitent, "such words shall share
This breath no more; devoted now to prayer.
O! if Thou seest (thine eye the future sees)
That I shall yet again blaspheme, like these;
Now strike me to the ground on which I kneel,
Ere yet this heart relapses into steel;
Now take me to that heaven I once defied,
Thy presence, thy embrace!"—He spoke, and died!

TO THE REV. MR. NEWTON, ON HIS RETURN FROM RAMSGATE

That ocean you have late survey'd,
Those rocks I too have seen;
But I, afflicted and dismay'd,
You, tranquil and serene.

You from the flood-controlling steep
Saw stretch'd before your view,
With conscious joy, the threatening deep,
No longer such to you.

To me the waves, that ceaseless broke

Upon the dangerous coast,
Hoarsely and ominously spoke
Of all my treasure lost.

Your sea of troubles you have past,
And found the peaceful shore;
I, tempest-toss'd, and wreck'd at last,
Come home to port no more.

Oct. 1780.

LOVE ABUSED

What is there in the vale of life
Half so delightful as a wife,
When friendship, love, and peace combine
To stamp the marriage-bond divine?
The stream of pure and genuine love
Derives its current from above;
And earth a second Eden shows,
Where'er the healing water flows:
But ah, if from the dykes and drains
Of sensual nature's feverish veins,
Lust, like a lawless headstrong flood,
Impregnated with ooze and mud,
Descending fast on every side,
Once mingles with the sacred tide,
Farewell the soul-enlivening scene!
The banks that wore a smiling green,
With rank defilement overspread,
Bewail their flowery beauties dead.
The stream polluted, dark, and dull,
Diffused into a Stygian pool,
Through life's last melancholy years
Is fed with overflowing tears:
Complaints supply the zephyr's part,
And sighs that heave a breaking heart.

A POETICAL EPISTLE TO LADY AUSTEN

Dear Anna—between friend and friend
Prose answers every common end;
Serves, in a plain and homely way,
To express the occurrence of the day;

Our health, the weather, and the news;
What walks we take, what books we choose;
And all the floating thoughts we find
Upon the surface of the mind.
    But when a poet takes the pen,
Far more alive than other men,
He feels a gentle tingling come
Down to his finger and his thumb,
Derived from nature's noblest part,
The centre of a glowing heart:
And this is what the world, who knows
No flights above the pitch of prose,
His more sublime vagaries slighting,
Denominates an itch for writing.
No wonder I, who scribble rhyme
To catch the triflers of the time,
And tell them truths divine and clear,
Which, couch'd in prose, they will not hear;
Who labour hard to allure and draw
The loiterers I never saw,
Should feel that itching and that tingling,
With all my purpose intermingling,
To your intrinsic merit true,
When call'd to address myself to you.
    Mysterious are His ways whose power
Brings forth that unexpected hour,
When minds, that never met before,
Shall meet, unite, and part no more:
It is the allotment of the skies,
The hand of the Supremely Wise,
That guides and governs our affections,
And plans and orders our connexions:
Directs us in our distant road,
And marks the bounds of our abode.
Thus we were settled when you found us,
Peasants and children all around us,
Not dreaming of so dear a friend,
Deep in the abyss of Silver-End.
Thus Martha, e'en against her will,
Perch'd on the top of yonder hill;
And you, though you must needs prefer
The fairer scenes of sweet Sancerre,
Are come from distant Loire, to choose
A cottage on the banks of Ouse.
This page of Providence quite new,
And now just opening to our view,
Employs our present thoughts and pains
To guess and spell what it contains:

But day by day, and year by year,
Will make the dark enigma clear;
And furnish us, perhaps, at last,
Like other scenes already past,
With proof, that we, and our affairs,
Are part of a Jehovah's cares;
For God unfolds by slow degrees
The purport of his deep decrees;
Sheds every hour a clearer light
In aid of our defective sight;
And spreads, at length, before the soul,
A beautiful and perfect whole,
Which busy man's inventive brain
Toils to anticipate in vain.

   Say, Anna, had you never known
The beauties of a rose full blown,
Could you, though luminous your eye,
By looking on the bud descry,
Or guess with a prophetic power,
The future splendour of the flower?
Just so the Omnipotent, who turns
The system of a world's concerns,
From mere minutiæ can educe
Events of most important use;
And bid a dawning sky display
The blaze of a meridian day.
The works of man tend, one and all,
As needs they must, from great to small;
And vanity absorbs at length
The monuments of human strength.
But who can tell how vast the plan
Which this day's incident began?
Too small, perhaps, the slight occasion
For our dim-sighted observation;
It pass'd unnoticed, as the bird
That cleaves the yielding air unheard,
And yet may prove, when understood,
A harbinger of endless good.

   Not that I deem, or mean to call
Friendship a blessing cheap or small:
But merely to remark, that ours,
Like some of nature's sweetest flowers,
Rose from a seed of tiny size
That seem'd to promise no such prize;
A transient visit intervening,
And made almost without a meaning,
(Hardly the effect of inclination,
Much less of pleasing expectation,)

Produced a friendship, then begun,
That has cemented us in one;
And placed it in our power to prove,
By long fidelity and love,
That Solomon has wisely spoken;
"A threefold cord is not soon broken."

Dec. 1781.

THE COLUBRIAD

Close by the threshold of a door nail'd fast
Three kittens sat; each kitten look'd aghast.
I, passing swift and inattentive by,
At the three kittens cast a careless eye;
Not much concern'd to know what they did there;
Not deeming kittens worth a poet's care.
But presently a loud and furious hiss
Caused me to stop, and to exclaim, "What's this?"
When lo! upon the threshold met my view
With head erect, and eyes of fiery hue,
A viper, long as Count de Grasse's queue.
Forth from his head his forked tongue he throws,
Darting it full against a kitten's nose;
Who, having never seen, in field or house,
The like, sat still and silent as a mouse;
Only projecting, with attention due,
Her whisker'd face, she ask'd him, "Who are you?"
On to the hall went I, with pace not slow,
But swift as lightning, for a long Dutch hoe:
With which well arm'd I hasten'd to the spot,
To find the viper, but I found him not.
And, turning up the leaves and shrubs around,
Found only that he was not be found.
But still the kittens, sitting as before,
Sat watching close the bottom of the door.
"I hope," said I, "the villain I would kill
Has slipp'd between the door and the door-sill;
And if I make despatch, and follow hard,
No doubt but I shall find him in the yard:"
For long ere now it should have been rehearsed,
'Twas in the garden that I found him first.
E'en there I found him, there the full-grown cat,
His head, with velvet paw, did gently pat;
As curious as the kittens erst had been
To learn what this phenomenon might mean.

Fill'd with heroic ardour at the sight,
And fearing every moment he would bite,
And rob our household of our only cat
That was of age to combat with a rat;
With outstretch'd hoe I slew him at the door,
And taught him never to come there no more.

1782.

SONG. ON PEACE

Written in the summer of 1783, at the request of Lady Austen, who gave the sentiment.
Air—"My fond Shepherds of late."

No longer I follow a sound;
No longer a dream I pursue;
O happiness! not to be found,
Unattainable treasure, adieu!

I have sought thee in splendour and dress,
In the regions of pleasure and taste;
I have sought thee, and seem'd to possess,
But have proved thee a vision at last.

An humble ambition and hope
The voice of true wisdom inspires;
'Tis sufficient, if peace be the scope,
And the summit of all our desires.

Peace may be the lot of the mind
That seeks it in meekness and love;
But rapture and bliss are confined
To the glorified spirits above.

SONG

Also written at the request of Lady Austen.
Air—"The Lass of Pattie's Mill."

When all within is peace,
How nature seems to smile!
Delights that never cease
The livelong day beguile.
From morn to dewy eve

With open hand she showers
Fresh blessings, to deceive
And soothe the silent hours.

It is content of heart
Gives Nature power to please;
The mind that feels no smart
Enlivens all it sees;
Can make a wintry sky
Seem bright as smiling May,
And evening's closing eye
As peep of early day.

The vast majestic globe,
So beauteously array'd
In Nature's various robe,
With wondrous skill display'd,
Is to a mourner's heart
A dreary wild at best;
It flutters to depart,
And longs to be at rest.

VERSES SELECTED FROM AN OCCASIONAL POEM ENTITLED "VALEDICTION"

Oh Friendship! cordial of the human breast!
So little felt, so fervently profess'd!
Thy blossoms deck our unsuspecting years;
The promise of delicious fruit appears:
We hug the hopes of constancy and truth,
Such is the folly of our dreaming youth;
But soon, alas! detect the rash mistake
That sanguine inexperience loves to make;
And view with tears the expected harvest lost,
Decay'd by time, or wither'd by a frost.
Whoever undertakes a friend's great part
Should be renew'd in nature, pure in heart,
Prepared for martyrdom, and strong to prove
A thousand ways the force of genuine love.
He may be call'd to give up health and gain,
To exchange content for trouble, ease for pain,
To echo sigh for sigh, and groan for groan,
And wet his cheeks with sorrows not his own.
The heart of man, for such a task too frail,
When most relied on is most sure to fail;
And, summon'd to partake its fellow's woe,
Starts from its office like a broken bow.

Votaries of business and of pleasure prove
Faithless alike in friendship and in love.
Retired from all the circles of the gay,
And all the crowds that bustle life away,
To scenes where competition, envy, strife,
Beget no thunder-clouds to trouble life,
Let me, the charge of some good angel, find
One who has known, and has escaped mankind;
Polite, yet virtuous, who has brought away
The manners, not the morals, of the day:
With him, perhaps with her (for men have known
No firmer friendships than the fair have shown,)
Let me enjoy, in some unthought-of spot,
All former friends forgiven and forgot,
Down to the close of life's fast fading scene,
Union of hearts without a flaw between.
'Tis grace, 'tis bounty, and it calls for praise,
If God give health, that sunshine of our days!
And if he add, a blessing shared by few,
Content of heart, more praises still are due—
But if he grant a friend, that boon possess'd
Indeed is treasure, and crowns all the rest;
And giving one, whose heart is in the skies,
Born from above and made divinely wise,
He gives, what bankrupt nature never can,
Whose noblest coin is light and brittle man,
Gold, purer far than Ophir ever knew,
A soul, an image of himself, and therefore true.

Nov. 1783.

EPITAPH ON DR. JOHNSON

Here Johnson lies—a sage by all allow'd,
Whom to have bred may well make England proud,
Whose prose was eloquence, by wisdom taught,
The graceful vehicle of virtuous thought;
Whose verse may claim—grave, masculine, and strong—
Superior praise to the mere poet's song;
Who many a noble gift from heaven possess'd,
And faith at last, alone worth all the rest.
O man, immortal by a double prize,
By fame on earth—by glory in the skies!

Jan. 1785.

TO MISS C—, ON HER BIRTHDAY

How many between east and west
Disgrace their parent earth,
Whose deeds constrain us to detest
The day that gave them birth!
Not so when Stella's natal morn
Revolving months restore,
We can rejoice that she was born,
And wish her born once more!

1786.

GRATITUDE. ADDRESSED TO LADY HESKETH

This cap, that so stately appears,
With ribbon-bound tassel on high,
Which seems by the crest that it rears
Ambitious of brushing the sky:
This cap to my cousin I owe,
She gave it, and gave me beside,
Wreath'd into an elegant bow,
The ribbon with which it is tied.

This wheel-footed studying chair,
Contrived both for toil and repose,
Wide-elbow'd, and wadded with hair,
In which I both scribble and dose,
Bright-studded to dazzle the eyes,
And rival in lustre of that
In which, or astronomy lies,
Fair Cassiopeia sat:

These carpets so soft to the foot,
Caledonia's traffic and pride!
Oh spare them, ye knights of the boot,
Escaped from a cross-country ride!
This table, and mirror within,
Secure from collision and dust,
At which I oft shave cheek and chin
And periwig nicely adjust:

This moveable structure of shelves,
For its beauty admired and its use,

...d charged with octavos and twelves,
...e gayest I had to produce;
...here, flaming in scarlet and gold,
...y poems enchanted I view,
...nd hope in due time, to behold
...y Iliad and Odyssey too:

...is china, that decks the alcove,
...hich here people call a buffet,
...ut what the gods call it above
...as ne'er been reveal'd to us yet:
...ese curtains that keep the room warm
...r cool, as the season demands,
...ose stoves that for pattern and form
...em the labour of Mulciber's hands:

...l these are not half that I owe
...o one, from our earliest youth,
...o me ever ready to show
...enignity, friendship, and truth;
...or Time, the destroyer declared
...nd foe of our perishing kind,
...even her face he has spared,
...uch less could he alter her mind.

...hus compass'd about with the goods
...nd chattels of leisure and ease,
...ndulge my poetical moods
...n many such fancies as these;
...nd fancies I fear they will seem—
...oets' goods are not often so fine;
...he poets will swear that I dream
...Vhen I sing of the splendour of mine.

786.

LINES COMPOSED FOR A MEMORIAL OF ASHLEY COWPER, ESQ. IMMEDIATELY AFTER HIS DEATH, BY HIS NEPHEW WILLIAM OF WESTON

...arewell! endued with all that could engage
...ll hearts to love thee, both in youth and age!
...n prime of life, for sprightliness enroll'd
...Among the gay, yet virtuous as the old;

...n life's last stage, (O blessings rarely found!)
...leasant as youth with all its blossoms crown'd;

Through every period of this changeful state
Unchanged thyself—wise, good, affectionate!

Marble may flatter, and lest this should seem
O'ercharged with praises on so dear a theme,
Although thy worth be more than half supprest,
Love shall be satisfied, and veil the rest.

June, 1788.

ON THE QUEEN'S VISIT TO LONDON. THE NIGHT OF THE SEVENTEENTH OF MARCH, 1789

When, long sequester'd from his throne,
George took his seat again,
By right of worth, not blood alone,
Entitled here to reign,

Then loyalty, with all his lamps
New trimm'd, a gallant show!
Chasing the darkness and the damps,
Set London in a glow.

'Twas hard to tell, of streets or squares
Which form'd the chief display,
These most resembling cluster'd stars,
Those the long milky way.

Bright shone the roofs, the domes, the spires,
And rockets flew, self-driven,
To hang their momentary fires
Amid the vault of heaven.

So, fire with water to compare,
The ocean serves, on high
Up-spouted by a whale in air,
To express unwieldy joy.

Had all the pageants of the world
In one procession join'd,
And all the banners been unfurl'd
That heralds e'er design'd,

For no such sight had England's queen
Forsaken her retreat,
Where George, recover'd, made a scene
Sweet always, doubly sweet.

Yet glad she came that night to prove,
A witness undescried,
How much the object of her love
Was loved by all beside.

Darkness the skies had mantled o'er
In aid of her design—
Darkness, O Queen! ne'er call'd before
To veil a deed of thine!

On borrow'd wheels away she flies,
Resolved to be unknown,
And gratify no curious eyes
That night except her own.

Arrived, a night like noon she sees,
And hears the million hum;
As all by instinct, like the bees,
Had known their sovereign come.

Pleased she beheld, aloft portray'd
On many a splendid wall,
Emblems of health and heavenly aid,
And George the theme of all.

Unlike the enigmatic line,
So difficult to spell,
Which shook Belshazzar at his wine
The night his city fell.

Soon watery grew her eyes and dim,
But with a joyful tear,
None else, except in prayer for him,
George ever drew from her.

It was a scene in every part
Like those in fable feign'd,
And seem'd by some magician's art
Created and sustain'd.

But other magic there, she knew,
Had been exerted none,
To raise such wonders in her view,
Save love of George alone.

That cordial thought her spirit cheer'd,
And, through the cumbrous throng,

Not else unworthy to be fear'd,
Convey'd her calm along.

So, ancient poets say, serene
The sea-maid rides the waves,
And fearless of the billowy scene
Her peaceful bosom laves.

With more than astronomic eyes
She view'd the sparkling show;
One Georgian star adorns the skies,
She myriads found below.

Yet let the glories of a night
Like that, once seen, suffice,
Heaven grant us no such future sight,
Such previous woe the price!

THE COCK-FIGHTER'S GARLAND

Muse—hide his name of whom I sing,
Lest his surviving house thou bring
For his sake into scorn,
Nor speak the school from which he drew
The much or little that he knew,
Nor place where he was born.

That such a man once was, may seem
Worthy of record (if the theme
Perchance may credit win)
For proof to man, what man may prove,
If grace depart, and demons move
The source of guilt within.

This man (for since the howling wild
Disclaims him, man he must be styled)
Wanted no good below,
Gentle he was, if gentle birth
Could make him such, and he had worth,
If wealth can worth bestow.

In social talk and ready jest,
He shone superior at the feast,
And qualities of mind,
Illustrious in the eyes of those
Whose gay society he chose,

Possess'd of every kind.

Methinks I see him powder'd red,
With bushy locks his well-dress'd head
Wing'd broad on either side,
The mossy rosebud not so sweet;
His steeds superb, his carriage neat,
As luxury could provide.

Can such be cruel? Such can be
Cruel as hell, and so was he;
A tyrant entertain'd
With barbarous sports, whose fell delight
Was to encourage mortal fight
'Twixt birds to battle train'd.

One feathered champion he possess'd,
His darling far beyond the rest,
Which never knew disgrace,
Nor e'er had fought but he made flow
The life-blood of his fiercest foe,
The Cæsar of his race.

It chanced at last, when, on a day,
He push'd him to the desperate fray,
His courage droop'd, he fled.
The master storm'd, the prize was lost,
And, instant, frantic at the cost,
He doom'd his favourite dead.

He seized him fast, and from the pit
Flew to the kitchen, snatch'd the spit,
And, Bring me cord, he cried;
The cord was brought, and, at his word,
To that dire implement the bird,
Alive and struggling, tied.

The horrid sequel asks a veil;
And all the terrors of the tale
That can be shall be sunk—
Led by the sufferer's screams aright
His shock'd companions view the sight,
And him with fury drunk.

All, suppliant, beg a milder fate
For the old warrior at the grate:
He, deaf to pity's call,
Whirl'd round him rapid as a wheel

His culinary club of steel,
Death menacing on all.

But vengeance hung not far remote,
For while he stretch'd his clamorous throat,
And heaven and earth defied,
Big with a curse too closely pent,
That struggled vainly for a vent,
He totter'd, reel'd, and died.

'Tis not for us, with rash surmise,
To point the judgment of the skies;
But judgments plain as this,
That, sent for man's instruction, bring
A written label on their wing,
'Tis hard to read amiss.

May, 1789.

TO WARREN HASTINGS, ESQ. BY AN OLD SCHOOLFELLOW OF HIS AT WESTMINSTER

Hastings! I knew thee young, and of a mind,
While young, humane, conversable, and kind,
Nor can I well believe thee, gentle then,
Now grown a villain, and the worst of men.
But rather some suspect, who have oppress'd
And worried thee, as not themselves the best.

TO MRS. THROCKMORTON, ON HER BEAUTIFUL TRANSCRIPT OF HORACE'S ODE, "AD LIBRUM SUUM"

Maria, could Horace have guess'd
What honour awaited his ode
To his own little volume address'd,
The honour which you have bestow'd;
Who have traced it in characters here,
So elegant, even, and neat,
He had laugh'd at the critical sneer
Which he seems to have trembled to meet.

And sneer, if you please, he had said,
A nymph shall hereafter arise,
Who shall give me, when you are all dead,
The glory your malice denies;
Shall dignity give to my lay,

though but a mere bagatelle;
nd even a poet shall say,
othing ever was written so well.

b. 1790.

TO THE IMMORTAL MEMORY OF THE HALIBUT, ON WHICH I DINED THIS DAY, MONDAY, APRIL 26, 1784

Where hast thou floated, in what seas pursued
Thy pastime? when wast thou an egg new spawn'd,
Lost in the immensity of ocean's waste?
Roar as they might, the overbearing winds
That rock'd the deep, thy cradle, thou wast safe—
And in thy minikin and embryo state,
Attach'd to the firm leaf of some salt weed,
Didst outlive tempests, such as wrung and rack'd
The joints of many a stout and gallant bark,
And whelm'd them in the unexplored abyss.
Indebted to no magnet and no chart,
Nor under guidance of the polar fire,
Thou wast a voyager on many coasts,
Grazing at large in meadows submarine,
Where flat Batavia, just emerging, peeps
Above the brine—where Caledonia's rocks
Beat back the surge—and where Hibernia shoots
Her wondrous causeway far into the main.
—Wherever thou hast fed, thou little thoughtst,
And I not more, that I should feed on thee.
Peace, therefore, and good health, and much good fish,
To him who sent thee! and success, as oft
As it descends into the billowy gulf,
To the same drag that caught thee!—Fare thee well!
Thy lot thy brethren of the slimy fin
Would envy, could they know that thou wast doom'd
To feed a bard, and to be praised in verse.

INSCRIPTION FOR A STONE ERECTED AT THE SOWING OF A GROVE OF OAKS AT CHILLINGTON, THE SEAT OF T. GIFFARD, ESQ. 1790

Other stones the era tell
When some feeble mortal fell;
I stand here to date the birth
Of these hardy sons of earth.

Which shall longest brave the sky,
Storm and frost—these oaks or I?
Pass an age or two away,
I must moulder and decay,
But the years that crumble me
Shall invigorate the tree,
Spread its branch, dilate its size,
Lift its summit to the skies.
  Cherish honour, virtue, truth,
So shalt thou prolong thy youth.
Wanting these, however fast
Man be fix'd and form'd to last,
He is lifeless even now,
Stone at heart, and cannot grow.

June, 1790.

ANOTHER

For a stone erected on a similar occasion at the same place in the following year.

Reader! behold a monument
That asks no sigh or tear,
Though it perpetuate the event
Of a great burial here.

June, 1790.   Anno 1791.

TO MRS. KING

On her kind present to the author, a patchwork counterpane of her own making.

The bard, if e'er he feel at all,
Must sure be quicken'd by a call
Both on his heart and head,
To pay with tuneful thanks the care
And kindness of a lady fair,
Who deigns to deck his bed.

A bed like this, in ancient time,
On Ida's barren top sublime,
(As Homer's epic shows)
Composed of sweetest vernal flowers,
Without the aid of sun or showers,

For Jove and Juno rose.

Less beautiful, however gay,
Is that which in the scorching day
Receives the weary swain,
Who, laying his long scythe aside,
Sleeps on some bank with daisies pied,
Till roused to toil again.

What labours of the loom I see!
Looms numberless have groan'd for me!
Should every maiden come
To scramble for the patch that bears
The impress of the robe she wears,
The bell would toll for some.

And oh, what havoc would ensue!
This bright display of every hue
All in a moment fled!
As if a storm should strip the bowers
Of all their tendrils, leaves, and flowers—
Each pocketing a shred.

Thanks then to every gentle fair
Who will not come to peck me bare
As bird of borrow'd feather,
And thanks to one above them all,
The gentle fair of Pertenhall,
Who put the whole together.

August, 1790.

IN MEMORY OF THE LATE JOHN THORNTON, ESQ.

Poets attempt the noblest task they can,
Praising the Author of all good in man,
And, next, commemorating worthies lost,
The dead in whom that good abounded most.
   Thee, therefore, of commercial fame, but more
Famed for thy probity from shore to shore,
Thee, Thornton! worthy in some page to shine,
As honest and more eloquent than mine,
I mourn; or, since thrice happy thou must be,
The world, no longer thy abode, not thee.
Thee to deplore were grief misspent indeed;
It were to weep that goodness has its meed,

That there is bliss prepared in yonder sky,
And glory for the virtuous when they die.
   What pleasure can the miser's fondled hoard,
Or spendthrift's prodigal excess afford,
Sweet as the privilege of healing woe
By virtue suffer'd combating below?
That privilege was thine; Heaven gave thee means
To illumine with delight the saddest scenes,
Till thy appearance chased the gloom, forlorn
As midnight, and despairing of a morn.
Thou hadst an industry in doing good,
Restless as his who toils and sweats for food;
Avarice in thee was the desire of wealth
By rust unperishable or by stealth,
And if the genuine worth of gold depend
On application to its noblest end,
Thine had a value in the scales of Heaven
Surpassing all that mine or mint had given.
And, though God made thee of a nature prone
To distribution boundless of thy own,
And still by motives of religious force
Impell'd thee more to that heroic course,
Yet was thy liberality discreet,
Nice in its choice, and of a temper'd heat;
And, though in act unwearied, secret still,
As in some solitude the summer rill
Refreshes, where it winds, the faded green,
And cheers the drooping flowers, unheard, unseen.
   Such was thy charity: no sudden start,
After long sleep, of passion in the heart,
But stedfast principle, and, in its kind,
Of close relation to the Eternal Mind,
Traced easily to its true source above,
To him whose works bespeak his nature, love.
   Thy bounties all were Christian, and I make
This record of thee for the Gospel's sake;
That the incredulous themselves may see
Its use and power exemplified in thee.

Nov. 1790.

THE FOUR AGES (A BRIEF FRAGMENT OF AN EXTENSIVE PROJECTED POEM)

"I could be well content, allowed the use
Of past experience, and the wisdom glean'd
From worn-out follies, now acknowledged such,

To recommence life's trial, in the hope
Of fewer errors, on a second proof!"
   Thus, while grey evening lull'd the wind, and call'd
Fresh odours from the shrubbery at my side,
Taking my lonely winding walk, I mused,
And held accustom'd conference with my heart;
When from within it thus a voice replied:
   "Couldst thou in truth? and art thou taught at length
This wisdom, and but this, from all the past?
Is not the pardon of thy long arrear,
Time wasted, violated laws, abuse
Of talents, judgment, mercies, better far
Than opportunity vouchsafed to err
With less excuse, and, haply, worse effect?"
   I heard, and acquiesced: then to and fro
Oft pacing, as the mariner his deck,
My gravelly bounds, from self to human kind
I pass'd, and next consider'd—what is man.
   Knows he his origin? can he ascend
By reminiscence to his earliest date?
Slept he in Adam? And in those from him
Through numerous generations, till he found
At length his destined moment to be born?
Or was he not, till fashion'd in the womb?
Deep mysteries both! which schoolmen must have toil'd
To unriddle, and have left them mysteries still.
   It is an evil incident to man,
And of the worst, that unexplored he leaves
Truths useful and attainable with ease,
To search forbidden deeps, where mystery lies
Not to be solved, and useless if it might.
Mysteries are food for angels; they digest
With ease, and find them nutriment; but man,
While yet he dwells below, must stoop to glean
His manna from the ground, or starve and die.

May, 1791.

THE RETIRED CAT

A poet's cat, sedate and grave
As poet well could wish to have,
Was much addicted to inquire
For nooks to which she might retire,
And where, secure as mouse in chink,
She might repose, or sit and think.

I know not where she caught the trick—
  Nature perhaps herself had cast her
In such a mould philosophique,
  Or else she learn'd it of her master.
Sometimes ascending, debonnair,
An apple tree, or lofty pear,
Lodged with convenience in the fork,
She watch'd the gardener at his work;
Sometimes her ease and solace sought
In an old empty watering pot:
There, wanting nothing save a fan,
To seem some nymph in her sedan
Apparell'd in exactest sort,
And ready to be borne to court.
  But love of change, it seems, has place
Not only in our wiser race;
Cats also feel, as well as we,
That passion's force, and so did she.
Her climbing, she began to find,
Exposed her too much to the wind,
And the old utensil of tin
Was cold and comfortless within:
She therefore wish'd instead of those
Some place of more serene repose,
Where neither cold might come, nor air
Too rudely wanton with her hair,
And sought it in the likeliest mode
Within her master's snug abode.
  A drawer, it chanced, at bottom lined
With linen of the softest kind,
With such as merchants introduce
From India, for the ladies' use,
A drawer impending o'er the rest,
Half open in the topmost chest,
Of depth enough, and none to spare,
Invited her to slumber there;
Puss with delight beyond expression,
Survey'd the scene, and took possession.
Recumbent at her ease, ere long,
And lull'd by her own humdrum song,
She left the cares of life behind,
And slept as she would sleep her last,
When in came, housewifely inclined,
The chambermaid, and shut it fast;
By no malignity impell'd,
But all unconscious whom it held.
  Awaken'd by the shock (cried Puss)
"Was ever cat attended thus?

The open drawer was left, I see,
Merely to prove a nest for me,
For soon as I was well composed,
Then came the maid, and it was closed,
How smooth these 'kerchiefs, and how sweet!
O what a delicate retreat!
I will resign myself to rest
Till Sol, declining in the west,
Shall call to supper, when, no doubt,
Susan will come and let me out."

 The evening came, the sun descended,
And Puss remain'd still unattended.
The night roll'd tardily away,
(With her indeed 'twas never day,)
The sprightly morn her course renew'd,
The evening grey again ensued,
And puss came into mind no more
Than if entomb'd the day before.
With hunger pinch'd, and pinch'd for room,
She now presaged approaching doom,
Nor slept a single wink, or purr'd,
Conscious of jeopardy incurr'd.

 That night, by chance, the poet watching,
Heard an inexplicable scratching;
His noble heart went pit-a-pat,
And to himself he said—"What's that?"
He drew the curtain at his side,
And forth he peep'd, but nothing spied.
Yet, by his ear directed, guess'd
Something imprison'd in the chest,
And, doubtful what, with prudent care
Resolved it should continue there.
At length a voice which well he knew,
A long and melancholy mew,
Saluting his poetic ears,
Consoled him and dispell'd his fears:
He left his bed, he trod the floor,
He 'gan in haste the drawers explore,
The lowest first, and without stop
The rest in order to the top.
For 'tis a truth well known to most,
That whatsoever thing is lost,
We seek it, ere it come to light,
In every cranny but the right.
Forth skipp'd the cat, not now replete
As erst with airy self-conceit,
Nor in her own fond apprehension
A theme for all the world's attention,

But modest, sober, cured of all
Her notions hyperbolical,
And wishing for a place of rest
Any thing rather than a chest.
Then stepp'd the poet into bed
With this reflection in his head:

MORAL

Beware of too sublime a sense
Of your own worth and consequence:
The man who dreams himself so great,
And his importance of such weight,
That all around, in all that's done,
Must move and act for him alone,
Will learn in school of tribulation
The folly of his expectation.

1791.

THE JUDGMENT OF THE POETS

Two nymphs, both nearly of an age,
Of numerous charms possess'd,
A warm dispute once chanced to wage,
Whose temper was the best.

The worth of each had been complete
Had both alike been mild:
But one, although her smile was sweet,
Frown'd oftener than she smiled.

And in her humour, when she frown'd,
Would raise her voice, and roar,
And shake with fury to the ground
The garland that she wore.

The other was of gentler cast,
From all such frenzy clear,
Her frowns were seldom known to last,
And never proved severe.

To poets of renown in song
The nymphs referr'd the cause,
Who, strange to tell, all judg'd it wrong,
And gave misplaced applause.

They gentle call'd, and kind and soft,
The flippant and the scold,
And though she changed her mood so oft,
That failing left untold.

No judges, sure, were e'er so mad,
Or so resolved to err—
In short the charms her sister had
They lavish'd all on her.

Then thus the god, whom fondly they
Their great inspirer call,
Was heard, one genial summer's day,
To reprimand them all.

"Since thus ye have combined," he said,
"My favourite nymph to slight,
Adorning May, that peevish maid,
With June's undoubted right,

"The minx shall, for your folly's sake,
Still prove herself a shrew,
Shall make your scribbling fingers ache,
And pinch your noses blue."

May, 1791.

YARDLEY OAK

Survivor sole, and hardly such, of all
That once lived here, thy brethren, at my birth,
(Since which I number threescore winters past,)
A shatter'd veteran, hollow-trunk'd perhaps,
As now, and with excoriate forks deform,
Relics of ages! could a mind, imbued
With truth from heaven, created thing adore,
I might with reverence kneel, and worship thee.
   It seems idolatry with some excuse,
When our forefather druids in their oaks
Imagined sanctity. The conscience, yet
Unpurified by an authentic act
Of amnesty, the meed of blood divine,
Loved not the light, but, gloomy, into gloom
Of thickest shades, like Adam after taste
Of fruit proscribed, as to a refuge, fled.

Thou wast a bauble once, a cup and ball
Which babes might play with; and the thievish jay,
Seeking her food, with ease might have purloin'd
The auburn nut that held thee, swallowing down
Thy yet close-folded latitude of boughs
And all thine embryo vastness at a gulp.
But fate thy growth decreed; autumnal rains
Beneath thy parent tree mellow'd the soil
Design'd thy cradle; and a skipping deer,
With pointed hoof dibbling the glebe, prepared
The soft receptacle, in which, secure,
Thy rudiments should sleep the winter through.
  So fancy dreams. Disprove it, if ye can,
Ye reasoners broad awake, whose busy search
Of argument, employ'd too oft amiss,
Sifts half the pleasures of short life away!
  Thou fell'st mature; and, in the loamy clod
Swelling with vegetative force instinct,
Didst burst thine egg, as theirs the fabled twins,
Now stars; two lobes, protruding, pair'd exact;
A leaf succeeded, and another leaf,
And, all the elements thy puny growth
Fostering propitious, thou becamest a twig.
  Who lived when thou wast such? Oh, could'st thou speak,
As in Dodona once thy kindred trees
Oracular, I would not curious ask
The future, best unknown, but at thy mouth
Inquisitive, the less ambiguous past.
  By thee I might correct, erroneous oft,
The clock of history, facts and events
Timing more punctual, unrecorded facts
Recovering, and misstated setting right—
Desperate attempt, till trees shall speak again!
  Time made thee what thou wast, king of the woods;
And time hath made thee what thou art—a cave
For owls to roost in. Once thy spreading boughs
O'erhung the champaign; and the numerous flocks
That grazed it stood beneath that ample cope
Uncrowded, yet safe shelter'd from the storm.
No flock frequents thee now. Thou hast outlived
Thy popularity, and art become
(Unless verse rescue thee awhile) a thing
Forgotten, as the foliage of thy youth.
  While thus through all the stages thou hast push'd
Of treeship—first a seedling, hid in grass;
Then twig; then sapling; and, as century roll'd
Slow after century, a giant bulk
Of girth enormous, with moss-cushion'd root

Upheaved above the soil, and sides emboss'd
With prominent wens globose—till at the last
The rottenness, which time is charged to inflict
On other mighty ones, found also thee.
    What exhibitions various hath the world
Witness'd of mutability in all
That we account most durable below?
Change is the diet on which all subsist,
Created changeable, and change at last,
Destroys them. Skies uncertain now the heat
Transmitting cloudless, and the solar beam
Now quenching in a boundless sea of clouds—
Calm and alternate storm, moisture, and drought,
Invigorate by turns the springs of life
In all that live, plant, animal, and man,
And in conclusion mar them. Nature's threads,
Fine passing thought, e'en in their coarsest works,
Delight in agitation, yet sustain
The force that agitates not unimpair'd;
But worn by frequent impulse, to the cause
Of their best tone their dissolution owe.
    Thought cannot spend itself, comparing still
The great and little of thy lot, thy growth
From almost nullity into a state
Of matchless grandeur, and declension thence,
Slow, into such magnificent decay.
Time was when, settling on thy leaf, a fly
Could shake thee to the root—and time has been
When tempests could not. At thy firmest age
Thou hadst within thy bole solid contents
That might have ribb'd the sides and plank'd the deck
Of some flagg'd admiral; and tortuous arms,
The shipwright's darling treasure, didst present
To the four-quarter'd winds, robust and bold,
Warp'd into tough knee-timber, many a load!
But the axe spared thee. In those thriftier days
Oaks fell not, hewn by thousands, to supply
The bottomless demands of contest waged
For senatorial honours. Thus to time
The task was left to whittle thee away
With his sly scythe, whose ever-nibbling edge,
Noiseless, an atom, and an atom more,
Disjoining from the rest, has, unobserved,
Achieved a labour which had, far and wide,
By man perform'd, made all the forest ring.
    Embowell'd now, and of thy ancient self
Possessing nought but the scoop'd rind, that seems
A huge throat calling to the clouds for drink,

Which it would give in rivulets to thy root,
Thou temptest none, but rather much forbidd'st
The feller's toil, which thou couldst ill requite.
Yet is thy root sincere, sound as the rock,
A quarry of stout spurs and knotted fangs,
Which, crook'd into a thousand whimsies, clasp
The stubborn soil, and hold thee still erect.
  So stands a kingdom, whose foundation yet
Fails not, in virtue and in wisdom laid,
Though all the superstructure, by the tooth
Pulverized of venality, a shell
Stands now, and semblance only of itself!
  Thine arms have left thee. Winds have rent them off
Long since, and rovers of the forest wild
With bow and shaft have burnt them. Some have left
A splinter'd stump bleach'd to a snowy white;
And some memorial none where once they grew.
Yet life still lingers in thee, and puts forth
Proof not contemptible of what she can,
Even where death predominates. The spring
Finds thee not less alive to her sweet force
Than yonder upstarts of the neighbouring wood,
So much thy juniors, who their birth received
Half a millennium since the date of thine.
  But since, although well-qualified by age
To teach, no spirit dwells in thee, nor voice
May be expected from thee, seated here
On thy distorted root, with hearers none,
Or prompter, save the scene, I will perform
Myself the oracle, and will discourse
In my own ear such matter as I may.
  One man alone, the father of us all,
Drew not his life from woman; never gazed,
With mute unconsciousness of what he saw,
On all around him; learn'd not by degrees,
Nor owed articulation to his ear;
But, moulded by his Maker into man
At once, upstood intelligent, survey'd
All creatures, with precision understood
Their purport, uses, properties, assign'd
To each his name significant, and, fill'd
With love and wisdom, render'd back to Heaven
In praise harmonious the first air he drew.
He was excused the penalties of dull
Minority. No tutor charged his hand
With the thought-tracing quill, or task'd his mind
With problems. History, not wanted yet,
Lean'd on her elbow, watching time, whose course,

Eventful, should supply her with a theme....

1791.

TO THE NIGHTINGALE, WHICH THE AUTHOR HEARD SING ON NEW YEAR'S DAY

Whence is it that, amazed, I hear
From yonder wither'd spray,
This foremost morn of all the year,
The melody of May?

And why, since thousands would be proud
Of such a favour shown,
Am I selected from the crowd
To witness it alone?

Sing'st thou, sweet Philomel, to me,
For that I also long
Have practised in the groves like thee,
Though not like thee in song?

Or sing'st thou, rather, under force
Of some divine command,
Commission'd to presage a course
Of happier days at hand!

Thrice welcome then! for many a long
And joyless year have I,
As thou to-day, put forth my song
Beneath a wintry sky.

But thee no wintry skies can harm,
Who only need'st to sing
To make e'en January charm,
And every season spring.

1792.

LINES WRITTEN IN AN ALBUM OF MISS PATTY MORE'S, SISTER OF HANNAH MORE

In vain to live from age to age
While modern bards endeavour,
I write my name in Patty's page,
And gain my point for ever.

W. COWPER.
March 6, 1792.

SONNET TO WILLIAM WILBERFORCE, ESQ.

Thy country, Wilberforce, with just disdain,
Hears thee by cruel men and impious call'd
Fanatic, for thy zeal to loose the enthrall'd
From exile, public sale, and slavery's chain.
Friend of the poor, the wrong'd, the fetter-gall'd,
Fear not lest labour such as thine be vain.
Thou hast achieved a part; hast gain'd the ear
Of Britain's senate to thy glorious cause;
Hope smiles, joy springs, and, though cold caution pause
And weave delay, the better hour is near
That shall remunerate thy toils severe,
By peace for Afric, fenced with British laws.
Enjoy what thou hast won, esteem and love
From all the just on earth and all the blest above.

April 16, 1792.

EPIGRAM PRINTED IN THE NORTHAMPTON MERCURY

To purify their wine, some people bleed
A lamb into the barrel, and succeed;
No nostrum, planters say, is half so good
To make fine sugar as a negro's blood.
Now lambs and negroes both are harmless things,
And thence perhaps this wondrous virtue springs,
'Tis in the blood of innocence alone—
Good cause why planters never try their own.

TO DR. AUSTIN, OF CECIL STREET, LONDON

Austin! accept a grateful verse from me,
The poet's treasure, no inglorious fee.
Loved by the muses, thy ingenuous mind
Pleasing requital in my verse may find;
Verse oft has dash'd the scythe of Time aside,
Immortalizing names which else had died:

And O! could I command the glittering wealth
With which sick kings are glad to purchase health!
Yet, if extensive fame, and sure to live,
Were in the power of verse like mine to give,
I would not recompense his arts with less,
Who, giving Mary health, heals my distress.
  Friend of my friend! I love thee, though unknown,
And boldly call thee, being his, my own.

May 26, 1792.

CATHARINA: THE SECOND PART: ON HER MARRIAGE TO GEORGE COURTENAY, ESQ.

Believe it or not, as you choose,
The doctrine is certainly true,
That the future is known to the muse,
And poets are oracles too.
I did but express a desire
To see Catharina at home,
At the side of my friend George's fire,
And lo—she is actually come!

Such prophecy some may despise,
But the wish of a poet and friend
Perhaps is approved in the skies,
And therefore attains to its end.
'Twas a wish that flew ardently forth
From a bosom effectually warm'd
With the talents, the graces, and worth
Of the person for whom it was form'd.

Maria would leave us, I knew,
To the grief and regret of us all,
But less to our grief, could we view
Catharina the Queen of the Hall.
And therefore I wish'd as I did,
And therefore this union of hands:
Not a whisper was heard to forbid,
But all cry—Amen—to the bans.

Since, therefore, I seem to incur
No danger of wishing in vain
When making good wishes for her,
I will e'en to my wishes again—
With one I have made her a wife,
And now I will try with another,

Which I cannot suppress for my life—
How soon I can make her a mother.

June, 1792.

EPITAPH ON FOP, A DOG BELONGING TO LADY THROCKMORTON

Though once a puppy, and though Fop by name,
Here moulders one whose bones some honour claim.
No sycophant, although of spaniel race,
And though no hound, a martyr to the chace—
Ye squirrels, rabbits, leverets, rejoice,
Your haunts no longer echo to his voice;
This record of his fate exulting view,
He died worn out with vain pursuit of you.
   "Yes,"—the indignant shade of Fop replies—
"And worn with vain pursuit, man also dies."

August, 1792.

SONNET TO GEORGE ROMNEY, ESQ. ON HIS PICTURE OF ME IN CRAYONS

Drawn at Eartham in the 61st year of my age, and in the months of August and September, 1792

Romney, expert infallibly to trace
On chart or canvass, not the form alone
And semblance, but however faintly shown,
The mind's impression too on every face—
With strokes that time ought never to erase,
Thou hast so pencill'd mine, that though I own
The subject worthless, I have never known
The artist shining with superior grace.

But this I mark—that symptoms none of woe
In thy incomparable work appear.
Well—I am satisfied it should be so,
Since, on maturer thought, the cause is clear;

For in my looks what sorrow couldst thou see
When I was Hayley's guest, and sat to thee?

October, 1792.

MARY AND JOHN

If John marries Mary, and Mary alone,
'Tis a very good match between Mary and John.
Should John wed a score, oh, the claws and the scratches!
It can't be a match—'tis a bundle of matches.

EPITAPH ON MR. CHESTER, OF CHICHELEY

Tears flow, and cease not, where the good man lies,
Till all who knew him follow to the skies.
Tears therefore fall where Chester's ashes sleep;
Him wife, friends, brothers, children, servants weep—
And justly—few shall ever him transcend
As husband, parent, brother, master, friend.

April, 1793.

TO MY COUSIN, ANNE BODHAM

On receiving from her a network purse made by herself.

My gentle Anne, whom heretofore,
When I was young, and thou no more
Than plaything for a nurse,
I danced and fondled on my knee,
A kitten both in size and glee,
I thank thee for my purse.

Gold pays the worth of all things here;
But not of love;—that gem's too dear
For richest rogues to win it;
I, therefore, as a proof of love,
Esteem thy present far above
The best things kept within it.

May 4, 1793.

INSCRIPTION FOR A HERMITAGE IN THE AUTHOR'S GARDEN

This cabin, Mary, in my sight appears,

Built as it has been in our waning years,
A rest afforded to our weary feet,
Preliminary to—the last retreat.

May, 1793.

TO MRS. UNWIN

Mary! I want a lyre with other strings,
Such aid from heaven as some have feign'd they drew,
An eloquence scarce given to mortals, new
And undebased by praise of meaner things,
That, ere through age or woe I shed my wings,
I may record thy worth with honour due,
In verse as musical as thou art true,
And that immortalizes whom it sings.
But thou hast little need. There is a book
By seraphs writ with beams of heavenly light,
On which the eyes of God not rarely look,
A chronicle of actions just and bright;

There all thy deeds, my faithful Mary, shine,
And, since thou own'st that praise, I spare thee mine.

May, 1793.

TO JOHN JOHNSON, ESQ.

On his presenting me with an antique bust of Homer.

Kinsman beloved, and as a son, by me!
When I behold the fruit of thy regard,
The sculptured form of my old favourite bard,
I reverence feel for him, and love for thee:
Joy too and grief—much joy that there should be,
Wise men and learn'd, who grudge not to reward
With some applause my bold attempt and hard,
Which others scorn; critics by courtesy.
The grief is this, that, sunk in Homer's mine,
I lose my precious years, now soon to fail,
Handling his gold, which, howsoe'er it shine,
Proves dross when balanced in the Christian scale.
Be wiser thou—like our forefather Donne,
Seek heavenly wealth, and work for God alone.

May, 1793.

TO A YOUNG FRIEND

On his arriving at Cambridge wet when no rain had fallen there.

If Gideon's fleece, which drench'd with dew he found
While moisture none refresh'd the herbs around,
Might fitly represent the church, endow'd
With heavenly gifts to heathens not allow'd;
In pledge, perhaps, of favours from on high,
Thy locks were wet when others' locks were dry:
Heaven grant us half the omen—may we see
Not drought on others, but much dew on thee!

May, 1793.

ON A SPANIEL, CALLED BEAU, KILLING A YOUNG BIRD

A spaniel, Beau, that fares like you,
Well fed, and at his ease,
Should wiser be than to pursue
Each trifle that he sees.

But you have kill'd a tiny bird,
Which flew not till to-day,
Against my orders, whom you heard
Forbidding you the prey.

Nor did you kill that you might eat
And ease a doggish pain,
For him, though chased with furious heat,
You left where he was slain.

Nor was he of the thievish sort,
Or one whom blood allures,
But innocent was all his sport
Whom you have torn for yours.

My dog! what remedy remains,
Since teach you all I can,
I see you, after all my pains,
So much resemble man?

July 15, 1793.

BEAU'S REPLY

Sir, when I flew to seize the bird
In spite of your command,
A louder voice than yours I heard,
And harder to withstand.

You cried—Forbear!—but in my breast
A mightier cried—Proceed!—
'Twas nature, Sir, whose strong behest
Impell'd me to the deed.

Yet, much as nature I respect,
I ventured once to break
(As you perhaps may recollect)
Her precept for your sake;

And when your linnet on a day,
Passing his prison door,
Had flutter'd all his strength away,
And panting press'd the floor.

Well knowing him a sacred thing,
Not destined to my tooth,
I only kiss'd his ruffled wing,
And lick'd the feathers smooth.

Let my obedience then excuse
My disobedience now,
Nor some reproof yourself refuse
From your aggrieved bow-wow:

If killing birds be such a crime,
(Which I can hardly see,)
What think you, Sir, of killing time
With verse address'd to me!

TO WILLIAM HAYLEY, ESQ.

Dear architect of fine chateaux in air,
Worthier to stand for ever, if they could,

an any built of stone or yet of wood,
r back of royal elephant to bear!

for permission from the skies to share,
uch to my own, though little to thy good,
ith thee (not subject to the jealous mood!)
partnership of literary ware!

ut I am bankrupt now; and doom'd henceforth
o drudge, in descant dry, on others' lays;
rds, I acknowledge, of unequall'd birth!
ut what his commentator's happiest praise?

hat he has furnish'd lights for other eyes,
'hich they who need them use, and then despise.

ne 29, 1793.

NSWER

*o Stanzas addressed to Lady Hesketh, by Miss Catharine Fanshawe, in returning a Poem of Mr.
owper's, lent to her, on condition she should neither show it, nor take a copy.*

o be remember'd thus is fame,
nd in the first degree;
nd did the few like her the same,
he press might sleep for me.
o Homer in the memory stored
f many a Grecian belle,
Vas once preserved—a richer hoard,
ut never lodged so well.

793.

N FLAXMAN'S PENELOPE

he suitors sinn'd, but with a fair excuse,
Vhom all this elegance might well seduce;
Nor can our censure on the husband fall,
Who, for a wife so lovely, slew them all.

eptember, 1793.

TO THE SPANISH ADMIRAL COUNT GRAVINA

On his translating the Author's Song on a Rose into Italian Verse.

My rose, Gravina, blooms anew,
And steep'd not now in rain,
But in Castilian streams by you,
Will never fade again.

1793.

INSCRIPTION FOR THE TOMB OF MR. HAMILTON

Pause here, and think: a monitory rhyme
Demands one moment of thy fleeting time.
Consult life's silent clock, thy bounding vein;
Seems it to say—"Health here has long to reign?"
Hast thou the vigour of thy youth? an eye
That beams delight? a heart untaught to sigh?
Yet fear. Youth, ofttimes healthful and at ease,
Anticipates a day it never sees;
And many a tomb, like Hamilton's, aloud
Exclaims "Prepare thee for an early shroud."

EPITAPH ON A HARE

Here lies, whom hound did ne'er pursue,
Nor swifter greyhound follow,
Whose foot ne'er tainted morning dew,
Nor ear heard huntsman's halloo;

Old Tiney, surliest of his kind,
Who, nursed with tender care,
And to domestic bounds confined,
Was still a wild Jack hare.

Though duly from my hand he took
His pittance every night,
He did it with a jealous look,
And, when he could, would bite.

His diet was of wheaten bread
And milk, and oats, and straw;

Thistles, or lettuces instead,
With sand to scour his maw.

On twigs of hawthorn he regaled,
On pippins' russet peel,
And, when his juicy salads fail'd,
Sliced carrot pleased him well.

A Turkey carpet was his lawn,
Whereon he loved to bound,
To skip and gambol like a fawn,
And swing his rump around.

His frisking was at evening hours,
For then he lost his fear,
But most before approaching showers,
Or when a storm drew near.

Eight years and five round rolling moons
He thus saw steal away,
Dozing out all his idle noons,
And every night at play.

I kept him for his humour's sake,
For he would oft beguile
My heart of thoughts that made it ache,
And force me to a smile.

But now beneath this walnut shade
He finds his long last home,
And waits, in snug concealment laid,
Till gentler Puss shall come.

He, still more aged, feels the shocks,
From which no care can save,
And, partner once of Tiney's box,
Must soon partake his grave.

A TALE

In Scotland's realms, where trees are few,
Nor even shrubs abound;
But where, however bleak the view,
Some better things are found;

For husband there and wife may boast

Their union undefiled,
And false ones are as rare almost
As hedgerows in the wild—

In Scotland's realm forlorn and bare
The history chanced of late—
The history of a wedded pair,
A chaffinch and his mate.

The spring drew near, each felt a breast
With genial instinct fill'd;
They pair'd, and would have built a nest,
But found not where to build.

The heaths uncover'd and the moors
Except with snow and sleet,
Sea-beaten rocks and naked shores
Could yield them no retreat.

Long time a breeding-place they sought,
Till both grew vex'd and tired;
At length a ship arriving brought
The good so long desired.

A ship!—could such a restless thing
Afford them place of rest?
Or was the merchant charged to bring
The homeless birds a nest?

Hush—silent hearers profit most—
This racer of the sea
Proved kinder to them than the coast,
It served them with a tree.

But such a tree! 'twas shaven deal,
The tree they call a mast,
And had a hollow with a wheel
Through which the tackle pass'd.

Within that cavity aloft
Their roofless home they fix'd,
Form'd with materials neat and soft,
Bents, wool, and feathers mix'd.

Four ivory eggs soon pave its floor
With russet specks bedight—
The vessel weighs, forsakes the shore,
And lessens to the sight.

The mother-bird is gone to sea,
As she had changed her kind;
But goes the male? Far wiser, he
Is doubtless left behind.

No—soon as from ashore he saw
The winged mansion move,
He flew to reach it, by a law
Of never-failing love;

Then, perching at his consort's side,
Was briskly borne along,
The billows and the blast defied,
And cheer'd her with a song.

The seaman with sincere delight
His feather'd shipmates eyes,
Scarce less exulting in the sight
Than when he tows a prize.

For seamen much believe in signs,
And from a chance so new
Each some approaching good divines,
And may his hopes be true!

Hail, honour'd land! a desert where
Not even birds can hide,
Yet parent of this loving pair
Whom nothing could divide.

And ye who, rather than resign
Your matrimonial plan,
Were not afraid to plough the brine
In company with man;

For whose lean country much disdain
We English often show,
Yet from a richer nothing gain
But wantonness and woe—

Be it your fortune, year by year
The same resource to prove,
And may ye, sometimes landing here,
Instruct us how to love!

June, 1793.

TO MARY

The twentieth year is well nigh past
Since first our sky was overcast;
Ah! would that this might be the last!
My Mary!

Thy spirits have a fainter flo
I see thee daily weaker gro
'Twas my distress that brought thee low,
My Mary!

Thy needles, once a shining store,
For my sake restless heretofore,
Now rust disused, and shine no more;
My Mary!

For, though thou gladly wouldst fulfil
The same kind office for me still,
Thy sight now seconds not thy will,
My Mary!

But well thou play'dst the housewife's part,
And all thy threads with magic art
Have wound themselves about this heart,
My Mary!

Thy indistinct expressions seem
Like language utter'd in a dream:
Yet me they charm, whate'er the theme,
My Mary!

Thy silver locks, once auburn bright,
Are still more lovely in my sight
Than golden beams of orient light,
My Mary!

For, could I view nor them nor thee,
What sight worth seeing could I see?
The sun would rise in vain for me,
My Mary!

Partakers of thy sad decline,
Thy hands their little force resign;
Yet gently press'd, press gently mine,
My Mary!

Such feebleness of limbs thou provest,
That now at every step thou movest
Upheld by two; yet still thou lovest,
My Mary!

And still to love, though press'd with ill,
In wintry age to feel no chill,
With me is to be lovely still,
My Mary!

But ah! by constant heed I know,
How oft the sadness that I show
Transforms thy smiles to looks of woe,
My Mary!

And should my future lot be cast
With much resemblance of the past,
Thy worn-out heart will break at last,
My Mary!

Autumn of 1793.

THE CASTAWAY

Obscurest night involved the sky,
The Atlantic billows roar'd,
When such a destined wretch as I,
Wash'd headlong from on board,
Of friends, of hope, of all bereft,
His floating home for ever left.

No braver chief could Albion boast
Than he with whom he went,
Nor ever ship left Albion's coast
With warmer wishes sent.
He loved them both, but both in vain,
Nor him beheld, nor her again.

Not long beneath the whelming brine,
Expert to swim, he lay;
Nor soon he felt his strength decline,
Or courage die away:
But waged with death a lasting strife,
Supported by despair of life.

He shouted; nor his friends had fail'd
To check the vessel's course,
But so the furious blast prevail'd,
That, pitiless perforce,
They left their outcast mate behind,
And scudded still before the wind.

Some succour yet they could afford;
And, such as storms allow,
The cask, the coop, the floated cord,
Delay'd not to bestow:
But he, they knew, nor ship nor shore,
Whate'er they gave, should visit more.

Nor, cruel as it seem'd, could he
Their haste himself condemn,
Aware that flight, in such a sea,
Alone could rescue them;
Yet bitter felt it still to die
Deserted, and his friends so nigh.

He long survives, who lives an hour
In ocean, self-upheld:
And so long he, with unspent power,
His destiny repell'd:
And ever, as the minutes flew,
Entreated help, or cried—"Adieu!"

At length, his transient respite past,
His comrades, who before
Had heard his voice in every blast,
Could catch the sound no more:
For then, by toil subdued, he drank
The stifling wave, and then he sank.

No poet wept him; but the page
Of narrative sincere,
That tells his name, his worth, his age,
Is wet with Anson's tear;
And tears by bards or heroes shed
Alike immortalize the dead.

I therefore purpose not, or dream,
Descanting on his fate,
To give the melancholy theme
A more enduring date:
But misery still delights to trace
Its semblance in another's case.

No voice divine the storm allay'd,
No light propitious shone;
When, snatch'd from all effectual aid,
We perish'd, each alone:
But I beneath a rougher sea,
And whelm'd in deeper gulfs than he.
March 20, 1799.

TO SIR JOSHUA REYNOLDS

Dear President, whose art sublime
Gives perpetuity to time,
And bids transactions of a day,
That fleeting hours would waft away
To dark futurity, survive,
And in unfading beauty live,—
You cannot with a grace decline
A special mandate of the Nine—
Yourself, whatever task you choose,
So much indebted to the Muse.
  Thus say the sisterhood:—We come—
Fix well your pallet on your thumb,
Prepare the pencil and the tints—
We come to furnish you with hints.
French disappointment, British glory,
Must be the subject of the story.
  First strike a curve, a graceful bow,
Then slope it to a point below;
Your outline easy, airy, light,
Fill'd up, becomes a paper kite.
Let independence, sanguine, horrid,
Blaze like a meteor in the forehead:
Beneath (but lay aside your graces)
Draw six-and-twenty rueful faces,
Each with a staring, stedfast eye,
Fix'd on his great and good ally.
France flies the kite—'tis on the wing—
Britannia's lightning cuts the string.
The wind that raised it, ere it ceases,
Just rends it into thirteen pieces,
Takes charge of every fluttering sheet,
And lays them all at George's feet.
  Iberia, trembling from afar,
Renounces the confederate war.
Her efforts and her arts o'ercome,

France calls her shatter'd navies home.
Repenting Holland learns to mourn
The sacred treaties she has torn;
Astonishment and awe profound
Are stamp'd upon the nations round:
Without one friend, above all foes,
Britannia gives the world repose.

ON THE AUTHOR OF LETTERS ON LITERATURE

The Genius of the Augustan age
His head among Rome's ruins rear'd,
And, bursting with heroic rage,
When literary Heron appear'd;

Thou hast, he cried, like him of old
Who set the Ephesian dome on fire,
By being scandalously bold,
Attain'd the mark of thy desire.

And for traducing Virgil's name
Shalt share his merited reward;
A perpetuity of fame,
That rots, and stinks, and is abhorr'd.

THE DISTRESSED TRAVELLERS; OR, LABOUR IN VAIN

A New Song, to a Tune never sung before.

I sing of a journey to Clifton,
We would have performed, if we could;
Without cart or barrow, to lift on
Poor Mary and me through the mud.
Slee, sla, slud,
Stuck in the mud;
Oh it is pretty to wade through a flood!

So away we went, slipping and sliding;
Hop, hop, à la mode de deux frogs;
'Tis near as good walking as riding,
When ladies are dressed in their clogs.
Wheels, no doubt,
Go briskly about,
But they clatter, and rattle, and make such a rout.

DIALOGUE

SHE

"Well! now, I protest it is charming;
How finely the weather improves!
That cloud, though 'tis rather alarming,
How slowly and stately it moves."

HE

"Pshaw! never mind,
'Tis not in the wind,
We are travelling south, and shall leave it behind."

SHE

"I am glad we are come for an airing,
For folks may be pounded, and penn'd,
Until they grow rusty, not caring
To stir half a mile to an end."

HE

"The longer we stay,
The longer we may;
It's a folly to think about weather or way."

SHE

"But now I begin to be frighted,
If I fall, what a way I should roll!
I am glad that the bridge was indicted,
Stay! stop! I am sunk in a hole!"

HE

"Nay never care,
'Tis a common affair;
You'll not be the last, that will set a foot there."

SHE

"Let me breathe now a little, and ponder
On what it were better to do;
That terrible lane I see yonder,
I think we shall never get through."

HE

"So think I:—
But, by the bye,
We never shall know, if we never should try."

SHE

"But should we get there, how shall we get home?
What a terrible deal of bad road we have past!
Slipping, and sliding, and if we should come
To a difficult stile, I am ruined at last!
Oh this lane!
Now it is plain
That struggling and striving is labour in vain."

HE

"Stick fast there while I go and look;"

SHE

"Don't go away, for fear I should fall:"

HE

"I have examined it, every nook,
And what you see here is a sample of all.
Come, wheel round,
The dirt we have found
Would be an estate, at a farthing a pound."
Now, sister Anne, the guitar you must take,
Set it, and sing it, and make it a song:
I have varied the verse, for variety's sake,
And cut it off short—because it was long.
'Tis hobbling and lame,
Which critics won't blame,
For the sense and the sound, they say, should be the same.

STANZAS ON THE LATE INDECENT LIBERTIES TAKEN WITH THE REMAINS OF MILTON. ANNO 1790

"Me too, perchance, in future days,
The sculptured stone shall show,
With Paphian myrtle or with bays
Parnassian on my brow.

"But I, or ere that season come,
Escaped from every care,
Shall reach my refuge in the tomb,
And sleep securely there."

So sang, in Roman tone and style,
The youthful bard, ere long
Ordain'd to grace his native isle
With her sublimest song.

Who then but must conceive disdain,
Hearing the deed unblest
Of wretches who have dared profane
His dread sepulchral rest?

Ill fare the hands that heaved the stones
Where Milton's ashes lay,
That trembled not to grasp his bones
And steal his dust away!

O ill requited bard! neglect
Thy living worth repaid,
And blind idolatrous respect
As much affronts thee dead.

August, 1790.

TO THE REV. WILLIAM BULL

June 22, 1782.

My dear Friend,

If reading verse be your delight,
'Tis mine as much, or more, to write;
But what we would, so weak is man,
Lies oft remote from what we can.
For instance, at this very time
I feel a wish by cheerful rhyme
To soothe my friend, and, had I power,
To cheat him of an anxious hour;
Not meaning (for I must confess,
It were but folly to suppress)
His pleasure, or his good alone,
But squinting partly at my own.
But though the sun is flaming high
In the centre of yon arch, the sky,
And he had once (and who but he?)
The name for setting genius free,
Yet whether poets of past days
Yielded him undeserved praise.
And he by no uncommon lot
Was famed for virtues he had not;
Or whether, which is like enough,
His Highness may have taken huff,

So seldom sought with invocation,
Since it has been the reigning fashion
To disregard his inspiration,
I seem no brighter in my wits,
For all the radiance he emits,
Than if I saw, through midnight vapour,
The glimmering of a farthing taper.
Oh for a succedaneum, then,
To accelerate a creeping pen!
Oh for a ready succedaneum,
Quod caput, cerebrum, et cranium
Pondere liberet exoso,
Et morbo jam caliginoso!
'Tis here; this oval box well fill'd
With best tobacco, finely mill'd,
Beats all Anticyra's pretences
To disengage the encumber'd senses.
    Oh Nymph of transatlantic fame,
Where'er thine haunt, whate'er thy name,
Whether reposing on the side
Of Oroonoquo's spacious tide,
Or listening with delight not small
To Niagara's distant fall,
'Tis thine to cherish and to feed
The pungent nose-refreshing weed
Which, whether pulverized it gain
A speedy passage to the brain,
Or whether, touch'd with fire, it rise
In circling eddies to the skies,
Does thought more quicken and refine
Than all the breath of all the Nine—
Forgive the bard, if bard he be,
Who once too wantonly made free,
To touch with a satiric wipe
That symbol of thy power, the pipe;
So may no blight infest thy plains,
And no unseasonable rains;
And so may smiling peace once more
Visit America's sad shore;
And thou, secure from all alarms,
Of thundering drums and glittering arms,
Rove unconfined beneath the shade
Thy wide expanded leaves have made;
So may thy votaries increase,
And fumigation never cease.
May Newton with renew'd delights
Perform thine odoriferous rites,
While clouds of incense half divine

Involve thy disappearing shrine;
And so may smoke-inhaling Bull
Be always filling, never full.

EPITAPH ON MRS. M. HIGGINS, OF WESTON

Laurels may flourish round the conqueror's tomb,
But happiest they who win the world to come:
Believers have a silent field to fight,
And their exploits are veil'd from human sight.
They in some nook, where little known they dwell,
Kneel, pray in faith, and rout the hosts of hell;
Eternal triumphs crown their toils divine,
And all those triumphs, Mary, now are thine.

1791.

SONNET TO A YOUNG LADY ON HER BIRTH-DAY

Deem not, sweet rose, that bloom'st 'midst many a thorn,
Thy friend, tho' to a cloister's shade consign'd,
Can e'er forget the charms he left behind,
Or pass unheeded this auspicious morn!
In happier days to brighter prospects born,
O tell thy thoughtless sex, the virtuous mind,
Like thee, content in every state may find,
And look on Folly's pageantry with scorn.
To steer with nicest art betwixt th' extreme
Of idle mirth, and affectation coy;
To blend good sense with elegance and ease;
To bid Affliction's eye no longer stream;
Is thine; best gift, the unfailing source of joy,
The guide to pleasures which can never cease!

ON A MISTAKE IN HIS TRANSLATION OF HOMER

Cowper had sinn'd with some excuse,
If, bound in rhyming tethers,
He had committed this abuse
Of changing ewes for wethers;

But, male for female is a trope,

Or rather bold misnomer,
That would have startled even Pope,
When he translated Homer.

ON THE BENEFIT RECEIVED BY HIS MAJESTY, FROM SEA-BATHING IN THE YEAR 1789

O sovereign of an isle renown'd
For undisputed sway,
Wherever o'er yon gulf profound
Her navies wing their way,

With juster claims she builds at length
Her empire on the sea,
And well may boast the waves her strength,
Which strength restored to thee.

ADDRESSED TO MISS — ON READING THE PRAYER FOR INDIFFERENCE

And dwells there in a female heart,
By bounteous Heaven design'd,
The choicest raptures to impart,
To feel the most refined—

Dwells there a wish in such a breast
Its nature to forego,
To smother in ignoble rest
At once both bliss and woe!

Far be the thought, and far the strain,
Which breathes the low desire,
How sweet soe'er the verse complain,
Though Phœbus string the lyre.

Come, then, fair maid, (in nature wise,)
Who, knowing them, can tell
From generous sympathy what joys
The glowing bosom swell:

In justice to the various powers
Of pleasing, which you share,
Join me, amid your silent hours,
To form the better prayer.

With lenient balm may Oberon hence
To fairy land be driven,

With every herb that blunts the sense
Mankind received from heaven.

"Oh! if my sovereign Author please,
Far be it from my fate
To live unbless'd in torpid ease,
And slumber on in state;

"Each tender tie of life defied,
Whence social pleasures spring,
Unmoved with all the world beside,
A solitary thing—"

Some Alpine mountain, wrapt in snow,
Thus braves the whirling blast,
Eternal winter doom'd to know,
No genial spring to taste.

In vain warm suns their influence shed,
The zephyrs sport in vain,
He rears unchanged his barren head,
Whilst beauty decks the plain.

What though in scaly armour dress'd,
Indifference may repel
The shafts of woe—in such a breast
No joy can ever dwell.

'Tis woven in the world's great plan,
And fix'd by Heaven's decree,
That all the true delights of man
Should spring from sympathy.

'Tis nature bids, and whilst the laws
Of nature we retain,
Our self-approving bosom draws
A pleasure from its pain.

Thus grief itself has comforts dear
The sordid never know;
And ecstasy attends the tear
When virtue bids it flow.

For, when it streams from that pure source,
No bribes the heart can win
To check, or alter from its course,
The luxury within.

Peace to the phlegm of sullen elves,
Who, if from labour eased,
Extend no care beyond themselves,
Unpleasing and unpleased.

Let no low thought suggest the prayer,
Oh! grant, kind Heaven, to me,
Long as I draw ethereal air,
Sweet Sensibility!

Where'er the heavenly nymph is seen,
With lustre-beaming eye,
A train, attendant on their queen,
(Her rosy chorus) fly;

The jocund loves in Hymen's band,
With torches ever bright,
And generous friendship, hand in hand
With pity's wat'ry sight.

The gentler virtues too are join'd
In youth immortal warm;
The soft relations, which, combined,
Give life her every charm.

The arts come smiling in the close,
And lend celestial fire;
The marble breathes, the canvas glows,
The muses sweep the lyre.

"Still may my melting bosom cleave
To sufferings not my own,
And still the sigh responsive heave
Where'er is heard a groan.

"So pity shall take virtue's part.
Her natural ally,
And fashioning my soften'd heart,
Prepare it for the sky."

This artless vow may Heaven receive,
And you, fond maid, approve:
So may your guiding angel give
Whate'er you wish or love!

So may the rosy-finger'd hours
Lead on the various year,
And every joy, which now is yours,

Extend a larger sphere!

And suns to come, as round they wheel,
Your golden moments bless
With all a tender heart can feel,
Or lively fancy guess!

1762.

FROM A LETTER TO THE REV. MR. NEWTON, LATE RECTOR OF ST. MARY WOOLNOTH

Says the pipe to the snuff-box, I can't understand
What the ladies and gentlemen see in your face,
That you are in fashion all over the land,
And I am so much fallen into disgrace.

Do but see what a pretty contemplative air
I give to the company—pray do but note 'em—
You would think that the wise men of Greece were all there,
Or at least would suppose them the wise men of Gotham.

My breath is as sweet as the breath of blown roses,
While you are a nuisance where'er you appear;
There is nothing but snivelling and blowing of noses,
Such a noise as turns any man's stomach to hear.

Then, lifting his lid in a delicate way,
And opening his mouth with a smile quite engaging,
The box in reply was heard plainly to say,
What a silly dispute is this we are waging!

If you have a little of merit to claim,
You may thank the sweet-smelling Virginian weed,
And I, if I seem to deserve any blame,
The before-mention'd drug in apology plead.

Thus neither the praise nor the blame is our own,
No room for a sneer, much less a cachinnus,
We are vehicles, not of tobacco alone,
But of any thing else they may choose to put in us.

THE FLATTING MILL. AN ILLUSTRATION

When a bar of pure silver or ingot of gold

Is sent to be flatted or wrought into length,
It is pass'd between cylinders often, and roll'd
In an engine of utmost mechanical strength.

Thus tortured and squeezed, at last it appears
Like a loose heap of ribbon, a glittering show,
Like music it tinkles and rings in your ears,
And, warm'd by the pressure, is all in a glow.

This process achieved, it is doom'd to sustain
The thump after thump of a gold-beater's mallet,
And at last is of service in sickness or pain
To cover a pill for a delicate palate.

Alas for the poet! who dares undertake
To urge reformation of national ill—
His head and his heart are both likely to ache
With the double employment of mallet and mill.

If he wish to instruct, he must learn to delight,
Smooth, ductile, and even his fancy must flow,
Must tinkle and glitter like gold to the sight,
And catch in its progress a sensible glow.

After all he must beat it as thin and as fine
As the leaf that enfolds what an invalid swallows;
For truth is unwelcome, however divine,
And unless you adorn it, a nausea follows.

EPITAPH ON A FREE BUT TAME REDBREAST, A FAVOURITE OF MISS SALLY HURDIS

These are not dewdrops, these are tears,
And tears by Sally shed
For absent Robin, who she fears,
With too much cause, is dead.

One morn he came not to her hand
As he was wont to come,
And, on her finger perch'd, to stand
Picking his breakfast-crumb.

Alarm'd, she call'd him, and perplex'd
She sought him, but in vain—
That day he came not, nor the next,
Nor ever came again.

She therefore raised him here a tomb,
Though where he fell, or how,
None knows, so secret was his doom,
Nor where he moulders now.

Had half a score of coxcombs died
In social Robin's stead,
Poor Sally's tears had soon been dried,
Or haply never shed.

But Bob was neither rudely bold
Nor spiritlessly tame;
Nor was, like theirs, his bosom cold,
But always in a flame.

March, 1792.

SONNET, ADDRESSED TO WILLIAM HAYLEY, ESQ.

Hayley—thy tenderness fraternal shown
In our first interview, delightful guest!
To Mary, and me for her dear sake distress'd,
Such as it is, has made my heart thy own,
Though heedless now of new engagements grown;
For threescore winters make a wintry breast,
And I had purposed ne'er to go in quest
Of friendship more, except with God alone.
But thou hast won me; nor is God my foe,
Who, ere this last afflictive scene began,
Sent thee to mitigate the dreadful blow,
My brother, by whose sympathy I know
Thy true deserts infallibly to scan,
Not more to admire the bard than love the man.

June 2, 1792.

AN EPITAPH

Here lies one who never drew
Blood himself, yet many slew;
Gave the gun its aim, and figure
Made in field, yet ne'er pull'd trigger.
Armed men have gladly made
Him their guide, and him obey'd;

At his signified desire
Would advance, present, and fire—
Stout he was, and large of limb,
Scores have fled at sight of him!
And to all this fame he rose
Only following his nose.
Neptune was he call'd, not he
Who controls the boisterous sea,
But of happier command,
Neptune of the furrow'd land;
And, your wonder vain to shorten,
Pointer to Sir John Throckmorton.

1792.

ON RECEIVING HAYLEY'S PICTURE.

In language warm as could be breathed or penn'd
Thy picture speaks the original, my friend,
Not by those looks that indicate thy mind—
They only speak thee friend of all mankind;
Expression here more soothing still I see,
That friend of all a partial friend to me.

January, 1793.

ON A PLANT OF VIRGIN'S BOWER. DESIGNED TO COVER A GARDEN-SEAT

Thrive, gentle plant! and weave a bower
For Mary and for me,
And deck with many a splendid flower,
Thy foliage large and free.

Thou camest from Eartham, and wilt shade
(If truly I divine)
Some future day the illustrious head
Of him who made thee mine.

Should Daphne show a jealous frown,
And envy seize the bay,
Affirming none so fit to crown
Such honour'd brows as they,

Thy cause with zeal we shall defend,

And with convincing power;
For why should not the virgin's friend
Be crown'd with virgin's bower?

Spring of 1793.

ON RECEIVING HEYNE'S VIRGIL FROM MR. HAYLEY

I should have deem'd it once an effort vain
To sweeten more sweet Maro's matchless strain,
But from that error now behold me free,
Since I received him as a gift from thee.

STANZAS, ADDRESSED TO LADY HESKETH, BY A LADY

In returning a Poem, of Mr. Cowper's, lent to the Writer, on condition she should neither show it nor take a copy.

What wonder! if my wavering hand
Had dared to disobey,
When Hesketh gave a harsh command,
And Cowper led astray.

Then take this tempting gift of thine,
By pen uncopied yet!
But canst thou Memory confine,
Or teach me to forget?

More lasting than the touch of art,
Her characters remain;
When written by a feeling heart
On tablets of the brain.

COWPER'S REPLY

To be remember'd thus is fame,
And in the first degree;
And did the few, like her, the same,
The press might rest for me.

So Homer, in the mem'ry stor'd
Of many a Grecian belle,

Was once preserved—a richer hoard,
But never lodged so well.

LINES ADDRESSED TO MISS THEODORA JANE COWPER

William was once a bashful youth,
His modesty was such,
That one might say, to say the truth,
He rather had too much.

Some said that it was want of sense,
And others, want of spirit,
(So blest a thing is impudence,)
While others could not bear it.

But some a different notion had,
And at each other winking,
Observed, that though he little said,
He paid it off with thinking.

Howe'er, it happened, by degrees,
He mended, and grew perter,
In company was more at ease,
And dress'd a little smarter;

Nay, now and then, could look quite gay,
As other people do;
And sometimes said, or tried to say,
A witty thing or so.

He eyed the women, and made free
To comment on their shapes,
So that there was, or seem'd to be,
No fear of a relapse.

The women said, who thought him rough,
But now no longer foolish,
"The creature may do well enough,
But wants a deal of polish."

At length improved from head to heel,
'Twere scarce too much to say,
No dancing beau was so genteel,
Or half so dégagé.

Now that a miracle so strange

May not in vain be shown,
Let the dear maid who wrought the change
E'en claim him for her own!

TO THE SAME

How quick the change from joy to wo,
How chequer'd is our lot below!
Seldom we view the prospect fair;
Dark clouds of sorrow, pain, and care,
(Some pleasing intervals between,)
Scowl over more than half the scene.
Last week with Delia, gentle maid!
Far hence in happier fields I stray'd.
Five suns successive rose and set,
And saw no monarch in his state,
Wrapt in the blaze of majesty,
So free from every care as I.
Next day the scene was overcast—
Such day till then I never pass'd,—
For on that day, relentless fate!
Delia and I must separate.
Yet ere we look'd our last farewell,
From her dear lips this comfort fell,—
"Fear not that time, where'er we rove,
Or absence, shall abate my love."

LINES ON A SLEEPING INFANT

Sweet babe! whose image here express'd
Does thy peaceful slumbers show;
Guilt or fear, to break thy rest,
Never did thy spirit know.

Soothing slumbers! soft repose,
Such as mock the painter's skill,
Such as innocence bestows,
Harmless infant! lull thee still.

LINES
Oh! to some distant scene, a willing exile
From the wild roar of this busy world,

Were it my fate with Delia to retire,
With her to wander through the sylvan shade,
Each morn, or o'er the moss-embrowned turf,
Where, blest as the prime parents of mankind
In their own Eden, we would envy none,
But, greatly pitying whom the world calls happy,
Gently spin out the silken thread of life!

INSCRIPTION FOR A MOSS-HOUSE IN THE SHRUBBERY AT WESTON

Here, free from riot's hated noise,
Be mine, ye calmer, purer joys,
A book or friend bestows;
Far from the storms that shake the great,
Contentment's gale shall fan my seat,
And sweeten my repose.

LINES ON THE DEATH OF SIR WILLIAM RUSSEL

Doom'd, as I am, in solitude to waste
The present moments, and regret the past;
Deprived of every joy I valued most,
My friend torn from me, and my mistress lost;
Call not this gloom I wear, this anxious mien,
The dull effect of humour, or of spleen!
Still, still, I mourn, with each returning day,
Him snatch'd by fate in early youth away;
And her—thro' tedious years of doubt and pain,
Fix'd in her choice, and faithful—but in vain!
O prone to pity, generous, and sincere,
Whose eye ne'er yet refus'd the wretch a tear;
Whose heart the real claim of friendship knows
Nor thinks a lover's are but fancied woes;
See me—ere yet my destin'd course half done,
Cast forth a wand'rer on a world unknown!
See me neglected on the world's rude coast,
Each dear companion of my voyage lost!
Nor ask why clouds of sorrow shade my brow,
And ready tears wait only leave to flow!
Why all that soothes a heart from anguish free,
All that delights the happy—palls with me!

ON THE HIGH PRICE OF FISH

Cocoa-nut naught,
Fish too dear,
None must be bought
For us that are here:

No lobster on earth,
That ever I saw,
To me would be worth
Sixpence a claw.

So, dear madam, wait
Till fish can be got
At a reas'nable rate,
Whether lobster or not;

Till the French and the Dutch
Have quitted the seas,
And then send as much
And as oft as you please.

TO MRS. NEWTON

A noble theme demands a noble verse,
In such I thank you for your fine oysters.
The barrel was magnificently large,
But, being sent to Olney at free charge,
Was not inserted in the driver's list,
And therefore overlook'd, forgot, or miss'd;
For, when the messenger whom we despatch'd
Inquir'd for oysters, Hob his noddle scratch'd;
Denying that his wagon or his wain
Did any such commodity contain.
In consequence of which, your welcome boon
Did not arrive till yesterday at noon;
In consequence of which some chanc'd to die,
And some, though very sweet, were very dry.
Now Madam says, (and what she says must still
Deserve attention, say she what she will,)
That what we call the diligence, be-case
It goes to London with a swifter pace,
Would better suit the carriage of your gift,
Returning downward with a pace as swift;
And therefore recommends it with this aim—
To save at least three days,—the price the same;

For though it will not carry or convey
For less than twelve pence, send whate'er you may,
For oysters bred upon the salt sea-shore,
Pack'd in a barrel, they will charge no more.

News have I none that I can deign to write,
Save that it rain'd prodigiously last night;
And that ourselves were, at the seventh hour,
Caught in the first beginning of the show'r;
But walking, running, and with much ado,
Got home—just time enough to be wet through,
Yet both are well, and, wond'rous to be told,
Soused as we were, we yet have caught no cold;
And wishing just the same good hap to you,
We say, good Madam, and good Sir, adieu!

VERSES PRINTED BY HIMSELF ON A FLOOD AT OLNEY

To watch the storms, and hear the sky
Give all our almanacks the lie;
To shake with cold, and see the plains
In autumn drown'd with wintry rains;
'Tis thus I spend my moments here,
And wish myself a Dutch mynheer;
I then should have no need of wit;
For lumpish Hollander unfit!
Nor should I then repine at mud,
Or meadows deluged with a flood;
But in a bog live well content,
And find it just my element;
Should be a clod, and not a man;
Nor wish in vain for Sister Ann,
With charitable aid to drag
My mind out of its proper quag;
Should have the genius of a boor,
And no ambition to have more.

EXTRACT FROM A SUNDAY-SCHOOL HYMN

Hear, Lord, the song of praise and pray'r,
In heaven, thy dwelling-place,
From infants, made the public care,
And taught to seek thy face!

Thanks for thy word, and for thy day,
And grant us, we implore,
Never to waste in sinful play
Thy holy sabbaths more.

Thanks that we hear—but, oh! impart
To each desires sincere,
That we may listen with our heart,
And learn, as well as hear.

ON THE RECEIPT OF A HAMPER. (IN THE MANNER OF HOMER)

The straw-stuff'd hamper with his ruthless steel
He open'd, cutting sheer th' inserted cords
Which bound the lid and lip secure. Forth came
The rustling package first, bright straw of wheat,
Or oats, or barley; next a bottle green
Throat-full, clear spirits the contents, distill'd
Drop after drop odorous, by the art
Of the fair mother of his friend—the Rose.

ON THE NEGLECT OF HOMER

Could Homer come himself, distress'd and poor,
And tune his harp at Rhedicina's door,
The rich old vixen would exclaim, (I fear,)
Begone! no tramper gets a farthing here."

William Cowper – A Short Biography

William Cowper was born 26th November 1731 in Berkhamsted, Hertfordshire, where his father John Cowper was the rector of the Church of St Peter. His mother was Ann née Donne (a relative of the great poet, John Donne). Only Cowper, the eldest child, and his brother John, out of seven children, survived past infancy. Ann died giving birth to John on 7th November 1737. His mother's death when he was only six was deeply traumatising to the young Cowper. Indeed, a half century later it was used as the basis of his poem, 'On the Receipt of My Mother's Picture'. The tragedy did however draw him closer to the rest of her side of the family. He was particularly close with his uncle Robert and his wife Harriot. It was their influence that engendered in him a love of reading, and their literary gifts, John Bunyan's Pilgrim's Progress and John Gay's Fables, opened his eyes to the world of writing.

After moving from school to school for several years he was, in the April of 1742, enrolled into Westminster school, popular at the time amongst prominent Whig supporting families. Cowper made many lifetime friendships at the school as well as a devotion to Latin which he later used in his poetry translations as well as his own verse.

Particularly at Westminster he read and was inspired by Homer's 'The Iliad' and 'The Odyssey'. His later translations of both works were often regarded as seminal.

After leaving Westminster Cowper was articled to Mr Chapman, solicitor, of Ely Place, Holborn, for training in the legal profession. During this period his leisure time was spent at his uncle Robert's home where he fell in love with his cousin, Theodora. However Robert thought that the marriage of persons so closely related was improper and refused the pleas of both nephew and daughter. Cowper took the decision particularly hard.

In 1763 he was offered a Clerkship of Journals in the House of Lords. With the examinations approaching Cowper had a mental breakdown. He tried to commit suicide three times and a period of depression and insanity seemed to settle on him. He was sent to Nathaniel Cotton's asylum at St. Albans for recovery. It was in the aftermath of one suicide attempt that he wrote the poem 'Hatred and vengeance, my eternal portions' (often referred to as 'Sapphics') was written. The end of this unhappy period saw him find refuge in fervent evangelical Christianity, and it was also the inspiration behind his much-loved hymns.

After recovering, he settled at Huntingdon with the retired clergyman Morley Unwin and his wife Mary. Cowper became such good friends with them both that he moved into their house and then with them when they moved to Olney. It was there he met a former captain of a slave ship, now curate, who had now devoted his life to the gospel; John Newton. Shortly afterwards Morley Unwin fell from his horse and died. Cowper continued to live in the Unwin home and became even closer to the widow Mary.

Newton invited Cowper to contribute to a hymnbook that he was compiling. The resulting volume, 'Olney Hymns', although not published until 1779 includes hymns such as 'Praise for the Fountain Opened' and 'Light Shining out of Darkness' which to this day remain some of Cowper's most familiar verses.

However dark forces were about to overwhelm Coper. In 1773, he experienced a devastating attack of insanity, believing that he was eternally condemned to hell, and that God was instructing him to make a sacrifice of his own life. With great care and devotion Mary Unwin nursed him back to health and, after a year, he began to recover.

In 1779, Newton had moved from Olney to London, their 'Olney Hymns' was published and once more Cowper began to write verse. Mary, wanting to keep Cowper's mind occupied, suggested that he write on the subject of 'The Progress of Error'. After writing a satire of this name, he wrote seven others. These poems were collected and printed in 1782 as 'Poems by William Cowper, of the Inner Temple, Esq.'

In 1781 Cowper had the good fortune to meet a sophisticated and charming widow named Lady Austen who inspired a new bout of poetry writing. Cowper himself tells of the genesis of what some have considered his most substantial work, 'The Task', in his "Advertisement" to the original edition of 1785:

...a lady, fond of blank verse, demanded a poem of that kind from the author, and gave him the SOFA for a subject. He obeyed; and, having much leisure, connected another subject with it; and, pursuing the

in of thought to which his situation and turn of mind led him, brought forth at length, instead of the
le which he at first intended, a serious affair—a Volume!

e volume also includes 'The Diverting History of John Gilpin', a notable piece of comic verse and a
em entitled 'Mary'.

wper and Mary Unwin moved to Weston Underwood, Buckinghamshire in 1786, having become close
his cousin and Theodora's sister, Lady Harriett Hesketh. He now began his translations from the
ginal Greek into blank verse of Homer's 'The Iliad' and 'The Odyssey'. These new translations,
blished in 1791, were the most significant English renderings of these epic and classic poems since
se of Alexander Pope earlier in the century.

ry Unwin died in 1796, plunging Cowper into a gloom from which he never fully recovered. He did
wever continue to revise his Homer for a second edition. Aside from writing the powerful and bleak
em, 'The Castaway', he penned some English translations of Greek verse and translated some of the
les of John Gay into Latin.

lliam Cowper was seized with dropsy (an old word for the medical condition edema, an accumulation
fluid in the body leading to swelling) and died on 25th April 1800.

is buried in the chapel of St Thomas of Canterbury, St Nicholas's Church, East Dereham. A window in
estminster Abbey also honours him.

wper was one of the most popular poets of his era and changed the direction of 18th-century nature
etry by writing of everyday life and scenes of the English countryside. He can be seen as a forerunner
Romantic poetry. Coleridge called him the 'the best modern poet', and William Wordsworth was
rticularly taken by his poem 'Yardley-Oak'. William Wilberforce, the driving force behind the abolition
slavery, referred to Cowper as 'his favourite poet'.

wper wrote a number of anti-slavery poems and was asked to write in support of the Abolitionist
mpaign. His poem 'The Negro's Complaint' (1788) rapidly became famous. He also wrote several other
ems on slavery, many of which attacked the idea that slavery made any economic sense.

illiam Cowper – A Concise Bibliography

ney Hymns (1779) (in collaboration with John Newton)
ems by William Cowper (1782)
e Task (1785)
e Diverting History of John Gilpin (1785)
omer's Iliad (1791) (A translation in blank verse from the Greek)
e Odyssey by Homer (1791) (A translation in blank verse from the Greek)

Made in the USA
Middletown, DE
28 December 2023

46938779R00087